HOW TO INSTALL
AIR RIDE SUSPENSION SYSTEMS

Kevin Whipps

CarTech®

CarTech®

CarTech®, Inc.
6118 Main Street
North Branch, MN 55056
Phone: 651-277-1200 or 800-551-4754
Fax: 651-277-1203
www.cartechbooks.com

Edit by Bob Wilson
Layout by Connie DeFlorin

ISBN 978-1-61325-580-3
Item No. SA500

Library of Congress Cataloging-in-Publication Data Available

Written, edited, designed, and printed in the U.S.A.
10 9 8 7 6 5 4 3 2 1

DISTRIBUTION BY:

Europe
PGUK
63 Hatton Garden
London EC1N 8LE, England
Phone: 020 7061 1980 • Fax: 020 7242 3725
www.pguk.co.uk

Australia
Renniks Publications Ltd.
3/37-39 Green Street
Banksmeadow, NSW 2109, Australia
Phone: 2 9695 7055 • Fax: 2 9695 7355
www.renniks.com

Canada
Login Canada
300 Saulteaux Crescent
Winnipeg, MB, R3J 3T2 Canada
Phone: 800 665 1148 • Fax: 800 665 0103
www.lb.ca

S·A
S-A DESIGN

DEDICATION

For my son, K. J., who made me a better man.
For my daughter, Kaylee, who made me a better person.
And for my wife, Kirsten, who makes me whole.
I love you all.

ACKNOWLEDGMENTS

The funny thing about these books is how they come together. You'd think that it's just one guy sitting in front of a keyboard, hammering out notes until it all gets done. However, that's often far from the case. Instead, it's a team effort, and without everyone else, there's no way that I could get this done.

Seth McAtee is the owner of Switch Suspension and my friend. He helped me along the way with my other books, but when it came time to work on this one, I knew he would be a good guy to know. Seth let me into his shop so I could play with fittings, take pictures of air line, and just fiddle around. Toward the end, both he and his team were very patient with me when I invaded their shop for two weeks while I photographed one of their projects. Seth is also one of the nicest guys I know and is very easy to work with. So, to Seth, thanks.

Now, I just mentioned Switch Suspension, and you'd think that thanking Seth would be enough. Nope. Tom Parkinson has also saved my bacon on more than a few occasions and was always there to answer any question. James and Jason were both critical during the 1958 Impala build featured in Chapter 11. Those two are true professionals. Although I don't work with the rest of the team over there very often, they're all rock stars, and I very much appreciate what they do.

I've known Todd Burton at Lowboy Motorsports for a long time now—he was even a groomsman in my wedding. When it comes to air suspension and suspension in general, he's the guy. (He's also the king of duallies around these parts, so if you need wheels or suspension components, he's your huckleberry.) Todd and I did a lot of work on my 1995 Chevy back in the day, and a lot of those photos found their way into this book. He was pretty upset when I sold that truck, and rightfully so, but hopefully its inclusion here helps remove the sting a bit. Todd is a class act and a pro, and I wouldn't hesitate to recommend his shop to anybody.

Jason at Arizona High Test is a professional. I first met him when he worked for Seth at Switch Suspension, and we teamed up on a bunch of tech articles. When he struck out on his own to start a shop that focused mainly on chassis and wiring work, I worried that he might have honed in on too tight a market. However, his work is amazing, and, as a result, people from all over the country bring him their frames to make them perfect. Business is thriving. He was instrumental in helping me with the hard line portion of the book as well as so many other little things here and there. If you need chassis work done, an LS wired, or just need

HOW TO INSTALL AIR RIDE SUSPENSION SYSTEMS

someone to plumb your setup, he's your guy.

Lonnie Thompson is an interesting addition to this book. When I was writing *How to Restore Your Chevy Truck: 1973–1987*, I had a problem: trucks don't rust in Arizona. At least they don't rust like they do in Portland, Oregon, where Lonnie and Carolina Kustoms call home. So, I cold called him one day, and while on a visit there with my family, he let me into his shop. Soon, he was sending files to me like crazy—more than 3,000 of them, I think—and that helped me out a ton on both the 1973–1987 book, as well as *How to Restore Your Chevy Truck: 1967–1972*. That guy is an invaluable resource,

and I want to thank him a ton for his help here too.

I've never met Jayson Pang. But while researching Chapter 1, I spent a ton of time going through my old photo albums from my time in the mini-truck world. Along the way, I found pictures of the *Mclean Cruiser*, a Toyota pickup built in the pages of *Mini Truckin'* magazine back in the 1990s, but I didn't know the owner. So, I called another great guy, Juan Trevino, who I've known for close to 20 years now. Not only did Juan know all these great details that made it into the book but he also knew Jayson, who built the *Mclean Cruiser* at his old job *and* owned the very first Toyota pickup on airbags. Another weird twist was that I had a

picture of said truck in my scrapbook from 1994. Jayson and I spoke for over an hour one Sunday, talking about trucks and the "good old days." He was a big help on the book and a resource I hope to use again in the future.

If I hadn't made it clear already, Juan is also a rock star, and he also deserves a big thanks.

I have a day job, and for a good portion of the creation of this book, I had a boss who was very understanding. He let me take time off to cover installs and even encouraged me to pursue this project. His name is Jeff Trumpold. Even though he's no longer my manager, he's an amazing individual and someone I'm glad to call my friend.

INTRODUCTION

If you told the Kevin Whipps of 1999 that he'd be writing a book about airbags, he'd have told you to pound sand or, more likely, something with a lot more curse words. That's because 1999 Kevin was all about hydraulics. It was his preferred method of lifting his cars up and down. He even had a custom license plate that showed off his hatred for airbags, and that plate may or may not have snuck in a four-letter word.

Oh, to be in your 20s again.

Today, I still love hydraulics. However, the fact is that airbags are a cleaner, easier, and more reliable way to lift your car or truck up and down.

I first learned that in 2004. Back then, I had a 2001 GMC Sierra with a four-pump hydraulic setup that was pretty amazing, but it also spent a lot of time sitting because either I was too deep into the custom body work or the hydraulics weren't working. So, as one does, I bought another truck and doubled down. This time, it was a bone-stock 2004 Chevrolet Silverado with a V-6. Shortly after I bought it, I started cutting into it, making it a cool truck that laid frame and, eventually, body on airbags.

Even though I enjoyed hydraulics, airbags were the logical choice at the time. I had sponsors for the

project, and since everything I got was more or less free, it made a lot of sense to use it for what was mostly my daily driver. Back then, I had a few problems here and there but nothing crazy. When a line blew out on the freeway, I was okay because I plumbed check valves into my system, which meant that I wasn't left stranded. Aside from that, nothing bag related happened. I just drove the thing regularly to work and back and even from my home in Arizona to California and Las Vegas. It was great.

So, when my next build (a 1995 Chevrolet Silverado) came up, I decided to do the same thing. Over the course of a few weeks, my buddy Todd at Lowboy Motorsports and I (mostly Todd) did a stock-floor body drop on the Chevy and bagged it. Selling it is one of my biggest regrets because it was the perfect truck. It rode great, had zero problems, and looked beautiful just the way it was. I didn't need custom paint or anything to make it cool. It just *was* cool.

Since then, I haven't looked back. I recently picked up a white 1997 Chevrolet Silverado Centurion, which looks just like my 1995 Silverado with the addition of two extra doors. What's the plan? Bag it, of course. At this point, it's the obvious thing to do.

Things have gotten so much better too. When I first started messing around with cars in 1993, I had a buddy who was looking to bag his Mazda pickup. Back then, the airbags themselves were a few hundred dollars each, and no one knew how to make them work in a truck. However,

they figured it out, and as the years went on, entire companies were founded on the premise that airbags were the superior method for adjustable suspensions, and they tweaked and tuned their kits.

Just the other day, a friend asked me about bagging his car. He was new to the whole scene and wasn't sure what to expect. Could I guide him through the process? Of course I could, but should I? He wasn't a mechanical guy, and if something went wrong, he certainly wouldn't know how to fix it.

Are airbags a safe bet?

Today? Yes, they are. Thanks to those companies and their advancements, I wouldn't hesitate bagging my wife's sedan, much less anything else. That's what this book is all about. It'll start by giving you a little bit of backstory about airbags, including where they came from, how they came to become so popular, etc. Then, I'll move into each component that makes up an airbag setup.

That way, you can learn what each one is and how important they are in the chain. Finally, we're going to bag some vehicles. They are full builds so that you can see everything that goes into the process from soup to nuts, as they say. By the end, you will have a solid understanding of how an airbag system works and what you'll need to complete yours. I love this stuff, and hopefully that shows.

When I was presented with the opportunity to write a book about air suspension, I didn't hesitate a bit. The fact is that I almost feel like this was the book I should've written before *How to Restore Your Chevy Truck: 1973–1987* and *How to Restore Your Chevy Truck: 1967–1972*. I'd almost dare to say that it's the book I was born to write.

How would 1999 Kevin feel about that statement?

Who cares? That dude is long gone.

Now, let's get to bagging some stuff.

THE HISTORY OF AIRBAGS

Airbags have been around a lot longer than most people think. Firestone introduced them to the world in 1934 and then patented them in 1938. The following year, Firestone patented Airide air springs. Later, those springs were used on busses, helping to manage the heavy weights that a loaded 84-passenger vehicle can hold. Trains were up next, helping to smooth out the ride on rail cars. However, the real innovations were yet to come.

You probably first saw airbags on a freeway while you drove past a semitruck. Back in the 1970s, Firestone made cab and seat springs that helped smooth out the ride of those long-haul vehicles, and today the same principle is in use. If you look toward the back of the cab on those trucks, you can often find a pneumatic spring of some form just like you can near the axles.

Soon, the idea expanded into the automotive aftermarket world as well as RVs. By the 1990s, it trickled down to the consumer world and mini truckers.

The mini truck community in the 1990s was a crazy place. People in their late teens and early 20s were expanding on the previously popular custom van scene and making cheap trucks cool by lowering them as far as possible. At first, the only option was hydraulics, which often left the vehicle with a stiff ride that was uncomfortable to say the least. (Years later, once accumulators were introduced to the hydraulics scene, the "rough riding" stigma went away). So, the alternative was air—but not airbags, not yet, anyway.

The first idea was air shocks, which were available for trucks at the local Pep Boys or AutoZone. These bolted into the stock location on the rear axle and (thanks to a Schrader valve that the owner could mount in the cab) could lift the back of the truck up and down albeit very slowly. Soon, custom shops across the U.S. experimented with air shocks up front, but the problem was pressure. It took too much to extend a single shock, and it was almost impossible on a full-size pickup. Torsion bars helped with lift on mini trucks, but it was an imperfect solution.

Look under the master cylinder on the right side of this photo taken in 1995 or 1996. The white part going vertically is an air shock, and it was the way the owner of this 1994 Toyota pickup lifted it.

The Southern California Mini Truck Scene

It's hard to understate how much the Southern California mini-truck world had to do with air-bagged suspensions. It was a different time (before the internet and the free flow of information that it provides), so people had to wait for magazines or personal videotapes to tell them what was happening in the world. However, in Southern California, the mini-truck scene was booming, and thanks to the magazines that also called the area their home, everyone knew it.

Jayson Pang worked at the Chop Shop with Brian Jendro, who was one of the leaders in the industry. Jayson had a Toyota pickup that first rolled on air shocks in 1991, and a year later, he doubled the front shocks to get a little bit more lift. Air shocks were readily available at any auto parts store. They were cheap and designed with eyelets on both ends, which made them more flexible for installation. In late 1992, Jayson and Brian went off to Mac's Air Springs and saw a 1973–1987 Chevy truck lifted in the air with huge RV-style airbags. One of them commented to the other, "Man, that'd be sweet to do on one of our trucks, but those things are just too big." If that's where the story ended, things would be a lot different today.

As it turns out, there was a rep from Firestone at the shop that day, and he overheard their conversation. He went to his car and returned with a pair of some of the first Firestone 25C airbags, and he gave them to the guys for free.

Brian and Jayson originally were going to install them on Brian's Toyota, but it was from a previous generation, so it didn't fit quite right. However, Jayson's truck was new and already had some custom work done up front. So, by the end of the day, they installed the first set of airbags in a Toyota pickup.

That scene back then was very competitive. Everyone was trying to have the lowest truck with the biggest wheels and the biggest body drop (where the body is lowered or channeled down over the frame so that the rockers and bedsides contact the ground), and that person usually wound up on the cover of a magazine. Guys such as Brian and Jayson were a big part of that world, and if it weren't for them and the rest of the Southern California scene, we might not be bagging vehicles today. ■

Known as the **Mclean Cruiser,** *this was one of the first bagged trucks out there. Built by the Chop Shop and featured in* **Mini Truckin'** *magazine, it ran wire wheels, which was a bit controversial at the time.*

This is Jayson Pang's Toyota pickup. It's the first Toyota that was ever put on airbags (Firestone 25Cs). This photo was taken in 1994 at Endless Summer, which was a popular truck run at the Colorado River in Parker, Arizona.

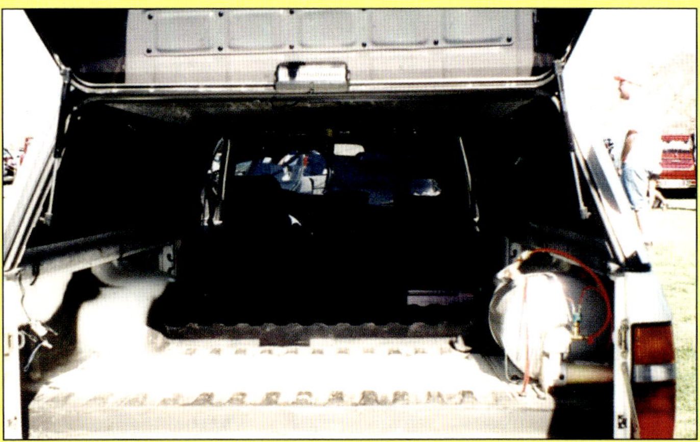

See that air tank and tiny compressor? That's everything that powered the air system in the **Mclean Cruiser** *back when this photo was taken in the 1990s. It took a long time to air up and fill the tank, but it worked, and that's all that mattered back then.*

This photo was taken in the mid-1990s, and you can see the gauge and valve setup of the time. Just one gauge showed the system status, while four ball valves put air into the shocks. If you look really closely, you can see the on/off toggle switch in the corner that was likely used to turn the air compressor on and off.

This 1990's-era air-equipped truck used ball valves and fittings to lift up and down. It was a cheaper and more accessible method back then (before valves and manifolds became commonplace).

Somewhere along the line—and it's debatable who was the first (see "The Southern California Mini Truck Scene" sidebar for more)—a mini-trucker took the airbag that was designed as a load leveler or something similar and installed it in their truck. They didn't have onboard compressors yet, and it was pretty crude, but it worked. The truck lifted up and down with ease.

The problem back then was the cost. Airbags could cost over $200 each, and when combined with the expensive air lines and fittings that people used back then, it was common to find a setup that cost upward of $4,000. Being a trendsetter was getting to be expensive.

However, as the late 1990s and early 2000s crept into view, a few things changed. For one, the price of airbag components dropped—supply and demand and all that. But in an interesting twist, the market for hydraulics began to dip as well. Throw in the added reliability and

This particular 1973–1980 Chevrolet C-30 pickup has a C-notch with an integrated airbag mount. Note that it still has the stock leaf springs. This is so that the leafs carry the bulk of the load, but when called upon, the airbags can provide extra support. (Photo Courtesy Switch Suspension)

distinct lack of oil found with airbags, and there was a scenario where the scene could flourish.

Now, this is how things happened in the custom car and truck world, which is likely why you picked up this book. However, there are many applications outside of building a car or truck to get low that can make the world go a little bit smoother.

The most common scenario is with load leveling. Airbags have been used for years as a way to add extra support in the back of a truck either for towing or when it's loaded down with extra cargo. You'll find either sleeve or double-convoluted models attached to the leaf spring pack on

This Suburban was modified to make access to the vehicle easier for the owner. It's not slammed, but the extra few inches of adjustability helps immensely. (Photo Courtesy Switch Suspension)

one end and the frame on the other. Either way, it's a great way to add some capacity to your vehicle.

Another option is with accessibility. If you're physically disabled and getting into a truck or SUV is difficult because of the extra height, adding airbags to lower it is not only convenient but also a huge advantage. It's a way to give yourself some mobility back, and that can be life changing.

In addition, there are many other creative applications for airbags. However, before diving into that, let's talk about the pros and cons.

Advantages and Disadvantages of Airbags

Let's get this obvious fact out of the way: having any kind of adjustable suspension on your vehicle makes it, by default, less reliable than something stock. Even cars and trucks with factory air-suspension systems are generally more reliable than aftermarket airbags, although nothing is ever bulletproof. The fact is that airbags can leave you on the side of the road if you put your system together improperly or even just miss a detail. However, when you do it the right way, it's magic.

Airbags are not perfect, but they're a lot better than the alternatives. Hydraulics require working with oil, regular maintenance, and (more often than not) a bank of batteries that put out a high voltage. Air cylinders came and went years ago, and air shocks are a joke to anybody who has a vehicle heavier than a late-1980s Honda Civic. Today, airbags are pretty much the de facto adjustable-height solution for any vehicle.

The advantages are huge, and the most obvious and talked-about one is ride quality. Cruising around in a vehicle that's properly set up on airbags is pretty amazing. Some liken it to floating on a cloud, while others compare it to the legendary Cadillac ride from the 1970s. In addition, it's also infinitely flexible. With a few tweaks and some stiffer shocks, you can turn any airbagged vehicle into a handling machine able to take the turns like a pace car. It's pretty cool. That's all thanks to the airbag's adjustable spring rate—more on that later.

The maintenance (or relative lack thereof) is also nice. Like anything on a vehicle, some routine service should be performed but nothing drastic. The details come later in the book, but to provide a teaser, it's basically emptying the air tank and regularly checking that nothing is rubbing or wearing funny. Seriously, it's that easy.

It's also a way to get your vehicle up and down. Although it's often seen as just a way to make your car, truck, or even motorcycle cooler, there are many scenarios where it's used to help the differently abled. A few years ago in the Phoenix, Arizona, area, there was a gentleman who had a Toyota Tundra on airbags. He was in a wheelchair, and he bagged his truck not only because of the cool factor but also for ease of entry. People with lifted trucks like them as well because it allows them to get into spots they couldn't previously because of their excessive height. In addition, when it comes to towing, they're an amazing load leveler, making the process a lot safer.

However, it's not always perfect. Airbags have their drawbacks, and they also go in pretty much the same sequence.

Although airbags ride great and can be tweaked for better handling, it's not always ideal for everyone in every scenario. For example, you might not want to take an airbagged GTO up Pikes Peak or use your laid-out Toyota on bags to deliver a bed full of newspapers.

Maintenance is minimal, but it's more than is needed with a stock vehicle. If you live in areas where

In the early days, there were two options: air shocks and hydraulics. Two pump/four dump hydraulic setups were available for less than $1,000, and air shocks just didn't get enough lift, so many turned to hydraulics (or "juice," as it was often called) for their up-and-down needs.

There was a stigma attached to hydraulics too. Since there were so many juiced cars that frequently had hydraulic problems, the other issue was reliability. Another option was needed.

Then, airbags came into the scene, and for a while, airbags and hydraulics were in real competition. While airbags rode well right out of the box, fans of hydraulics discovered accumulators—gas-filled balls that acted like shock absorbers for their cylinders. People talked smack to each other saying things that were either pro- or anti-airbags, and everyone took a side. It was nuts.

However, two things happened along the way that changed the game, and the way they happened almost simultaneously is magical.

The downside to airbags at the time was twofold. First, compressors were loud and slow, and no matter where you put them, they echoed and rattled, making them even louder. The second issue was one they shared with hydraulics: you never knew if your ride was physically level. With hydraulics, it was always guesswork: hit a few switches and hope that you weren't leaning to one side as you cruised. With airbags, you had gauges, but they didn't really help. It wasn't a dealbreaker by any means, but it was annoying.

The downsides to hydraulics were many. They required regular maintenance. Batteries had to be charged at least weekly. Cylinder seals needed to be replaced every few months (or even more frequently), and all that oil was messy to deal with. Plus, there was always the risk of a runaway—when a hydraulic motor continues turning after letting go of the switch. That was so dangerous that it led to fires, and that was scary. However, they got more lift than airbags and sure did look cool, so people stuck with it.

The first major shift came with AccuAir. Although it wasn't the first company to introduce something like this, AccuAir changed the game by perfecting height sensors that allowed the user to dial in the ride height perfectly. With push-button technology, it was easy to just get your ride and go, problem free. Plus, the compressors didn't have to cycle as frequently. When compressors got quieter and more efficient, that pretty much solved all the issues.

Meanwhile, hydraulic companies were dropping like flies. Legal troubles hit some of them, and others closed just prior to or during the Great Recession. The big boys in the industry went by the wayside, and soon it was just a few dedicated businesses that were willing to accept low-volume sales.

So, it came to a point where airbags became so reliable that it seemed silly not to run them, while hydraulics were becoming harder and harder to find, even if you wanted them. Today, hydraulics aren't dead, but they're definitely used primarily by dedicated fans.

No method of adjustable suspension is going to be 100-percent reliable. But in the war between hydraulics and airbags, airbags won. They did so because they've become as close to reliable as you can get. ■

This Ford Ranger was sponsored by Pro Hopper Hydraulics back in the mid-1990s but didn't have any of the expected lowrider look.

Meanwhile, this Ford Ranger, pictured at the same show, went with all airbags. It's the same generation of Ford Ranger too.

Looking further into the bed, it is apparent how truly custom and "mini-trucker-esque" the truck was. This was a show vehicle designed for hydraulics and to blow apart the mini-trucking scene, and it did.

the temperatures dip below freezing, you'll have to think about draining your tank(s) on a regular schedule and potentially deal with frozen valves. In addition, if you don't maintain things, it's simple enough to drag through an air line or break something ancillary to the bags (for example, wearing through bushings by overextending the suspension), which may mean you don't want to deal with it at all. Either way, it helps to be mechanically inclined when you have something on airbags.

Lifting your vehicle up and down has its pros and cons too. Most people don't adjust their suspension while driving, but if you do, check with your local laws because it may be illegal in your state. The same applies to things such as license plate and headlight heights, both of which are issues in California. If you do adjust on the go, having a problem at speed is a good way to wreck your ride.

All this is to say that although airbags are an amazing addition to any custom ride, you need to weigh the pros and cons along the way. If you don't own a basic toolkit and you have no idea how to turn a wrench, this might not be the ideal method of adjustable suspension for you. However, if you're handy or willing to learn, this could be perfect for your next project.

The "Cool" Factor

Having adjustable suspension carries with it a certain cool factor, and if you've ever owned it on one of your vehicles, you know exactly what that is. The feeling you get when you lay out your ride and you see heads swiveling your direction is priceless.

It's a somewhat indescribable feeling too. There's a combination of adrenaline and fear that rushes

If you go to any car or truck show, expect to see many rides on airbags. It's almost the standard now, and that's not a bad thing.

through your body as you're driving super low with the frame or body kissing the ground as you hit a bump. It's the way that you keep looking straight ahead but lay out your ride in a parking lot, knowing full well that heads are going to turn when they hear the air release. It's how when you're driving and you see kids staring from a nearby car, and you watch them flip out when you adjust the height in one direction or the other. It's pretty cool.

Airbags also occupy a weird place in the world of custom cars. Anyone who is in the scene knows about them, but if you're a regular civilian, it's a totally unheard-of concept. The best evidence of that is when you first drive your ride up to the cruising spot, park, lay it out, and a "normie" walks up to ask, "How do you drive that thing?" or the other popular one, "How do you get over a speedbump?" Regular people just don't know, and that makes it cool.

But it's also a rite of passage of sorts. Custom cars and trucks fall into a few categories. There's lifted or lowered, performance or show, import or domestic, and static or bagged. Static guys—those with suspensions that

stay the same all the time, whether they're lifted or lowered—are often working toward bagging their vehicle, or they're on a path that dictates not having any kind of adjustability outside of a coilover. Bagged people are different. They're the ones considered to be "extreme" compared to the rest. After all, they went the extra mile and spent the cash to get to this new level. It's a big deal.

If you're a truck enthusiast, bags are often considered standard. Yes, coilover suspensions have become more popular recently, but bags are (more often than not) the path to greatness.

Every year, the Specialty Equipment Marketing Association (SEMA) holds a huge event in Las Vegas with more than 150,000 attendees from the automotive industry. There are hundreds of cars, trucks, golf carts, and anything else on wheels there. How many of them are bagged? A lot—almost an inordinate amount. And the vehicles that everyone talks about after the show? Well, a lot of them are bagged. That's cool.

So, why should you install airbags on your ride? It's pretty clear by now, isn't it?

Reliability Issues

As has already been mentioned, there's no such thing as a 100-percent reliable adjustable suspension system. Something, at some point, can go wrong, and you need to be prepared for that eventuality, even if it just means carrying a AAA card for a tow. Today's modern tools and installation processes make for generally reliable setups, but if things were assembled incorrectly or user error occurs, you could find yourself in a pickle and need to get a way out.

What matters then is how you handle the problem.

First, start thinking about what the issue could realistically be. An air system is pretty straightforward (as you'll see in the next chapter), and there are only so many things that can go wrong. Not making air? It's either the compressor, air line, or the wiring leading to it. Not lifting? Could be the valves or a leak. Hearing a hissing noise? You have air coming out of somewhere. Hunt it down and fix it.

Then, start looking at the repair options. If you don't have a toolkit, you'll need to call a tow truck if you're blocking the roadway or just plain stuck. If not and it's more manageable, see what it'd take to limp it home. There are plenty of people who've dealt with a small leak on a four-hour drive home from a show, tapping the "up" switch all the way home. It happens.

However, the best thing you can do is be prepared. Know how your specific air system works and find ways to diagnose the problems if they come up. Think of every possible worst-case scenario and figure out a fix, plus bring the tools you'll need. By doing that, you'll always be prepared.

Lifted Trucks with Airbags

This book focuses mainly on lowered cars and trucks, but it's important to mention the rising contingent of lifted vehicles that are running airbags nowadays. It's not quite as common to see on the street, but they're out there, so let's take a moment to discuss the options.

When you see airbags on a lifted vehicle (typically a truck or SUV), there are a few reasons why. Usually they're severely lifted, meaning 12 inches or more. That makes it more difficult to enter and exit the vehicle. Airbags can help by lowering them to enter and lifting them to exit and be as high as possible.

Second, they're easier to install on extreme vehicles. Often, they have straight axles front and rear that are paired with either a multi-link suspension or leaf springs. Adding an airbag to that kind of setup is pretty straightforward, and since these trucks are often built for show, they enhance the look too.

Occasionally, airbags are installed on a lifted truck that's not built for show but instead off-roading. In these cases, the air-bags are used to shift weight around the vehicle and apply pressure when necessary. They can also be used as load levelers, particularly when pulling a trailer.

Whether you want to bag your lifted truck or not, many of the rules and tips throughout this book apply as well. The systems are all the same. The only difference is how you mount your airbags.

Motorcycles with Airbags

Similar to lifted trucks, I won't spend a lot of time talking about motorcycles on airbags, and that's mostly because many of them don't technically use airbags.

Motorcycles have a fork up front and sometimes a swingarm out back. As such, they usually have some kind of coilover shock involved in the back end, and that handles the ride and dampening.

For people who want air suspension in the rear of a bike, they usually get some variation of an air shock. After all, a motorcycle is much lighter than a truck, and it can handle the load just fine. Yes, occasionally someone custom builds a soft tail with a

Firestone airbag mount, but it's the exception and not the rule.

Up front, you also rarely see what you would call an airbag. Instead, there are modified forks and mounts that look like stock units but hold an air cylinder. They're very similar to airbags in that they hold air and can cycle up and down, but their construction is more like a hydraulic cylinder in that there's a piston with seals that provides the motion. There's no bag in most (but not all) of those kinds of setups.

So no, this book will not cover motorcycle airbags. But again, the

This was Craig Elder's 1999 Ford, which was built in the early 2000s. In the fenderwells, there are some huge airbags that he used to lift and lower the truck. Bags aren't only for people that are going low after all.

Carry a Toolkit

Nothing is worse than having your bagged vehicle break down and having to fix it on the side of the road.

This is a PTC union fitting, which is great if you have a puncture in your flexible air line. Just cut out the affected area and push each half of the line into the ends of the fitting. Just like that, it's fixed.

Although it's not entirely necessary to carry tools with you in your custom vehicle, it certainly doesn't hurt. There have been many times when someone experienced something unexpected while cruising, and if they only had the right tool on hand, they would've been able to fix it.

The best part is that you don't need a huge toolkit with you at all times. Instead, just be prepared for what could happen, and carry those kinds of tools with you.

Here are a few suggestions.

PTC Unions

If you have a line blow while driving, having a push-to-connect (PTC) union fitting on hand could save your day. Just cut out the section with the hole and splice in a new one with some PTC unions. You'll be back on the road in no time.

Spare Air Line

This one goes without saying. Have some spare line handy, and since it doesn't take up a lot of space, get concepts and applications are similar, and many things do cross over.

What Can and Can't Be Bagged?

On the surface, this is a pretty easy question. Almost anything can be bagged, and a quick search online will give you tons of results. Golf carts? Yup. Wheelchairs? Sure. There are a million different things that you can put on airbags. The difference, though, is what kind of airbag you use.

Double convoluted airbags (the kind you'll find in most vehicles) are designed to replace a spring. As such, it's made so that both ends are mounted to separate components, one of which is pivoted at some point. Think about the front suspension of a car—say, a 1958 Chevrolet Impala, which has a traditional A-arm setup (see Chapter 11). One half of the bag would sit in a cup inside the spring pocket, while the other half is bolted or mated to the lower control arm. As the bag inflates, it presses down on the suspension, pivoting the arm on the frame.

That basic concept (two pieces hinged on a pivot) is great for a double-convoluted airbag. You can do a ton of things with this premise. There's a company that makes a floor jack with an airbag on one end to lift a car super high. Many custom truck people cut a hole in their bed so they can create a cover over their bridge notch. Then, they build a cover and pivot one end so they can lift it with an airbag (or a pneumatic cylinder). Then, there are those who lift the entire bed with a pair of bags. There are many options.

The thing is that you can't use a double-convoluted airbag on everything because there's no structure to

enough to run the entire length of your vehicle just in case.

Spare Airbag(s)

One spare airbag is usually enough to take care of most jobs, but if you run different size bags, carry one of each. Then, you'll be prepared either way.

Air Line Cutter

Cutting air line isn't hard, but it has to be done straight. A specialized air line cutter makes that a lot easier. In addition, if you're installing a new line anyway, you're going to need something to cut it, so why not use the right tool?

Zip Ties

Everybody uses zip ties but feels shame in doing so. Forget about that. Just keep them handy for when you're in a bind. You can always remove the zip tie and fix it the right way when you get home.

Basic Tools

It's nothing too fancy, but keep the kind of tools on hand that you'd need for changing a tire and replacing an airbag: wrenches (a good crescent wrench always comes in handy), maybe a small socket set, etc. Make sure that you have the tools to remove a wheel so that you can access the suspension and fix or replace the airbag.

Air Line with Chuck

This is an item that you don't think about until you need it. If you have an extra port on your tank, consider installing an air line quick-disconnect fitting. Then, get a coiled air hose and put an air chuck on the other end or even just install another quick disconnect and carry an air chuck in your toolkit.

This does a few things. First, if your tire ever goes low, you have a built-in fix. Second, if you need air tools, you also have an air source (assuming you bring the right tools). Finally, it provides a way to fill up the tank if it goes empty and the compressor isn't working. It's not a glamorous item to install, but when it is needed, you'll love having it.

Spray Bottle with Water and Dish Soap

Why? A spray bottle with water and a few drops of dish soap is great for finding leaks. Spray the water onto the area where you think there may be a leak and look for bubbles. It's a surprisingly handy thing to have when you can hear air hissing but can't find the source.

Teflon Tape/Loctite 545

Always have some extra thread sealant handy, even if it's just Teflon tape. If you've found a leak at a fitting connection, the only way to tighten it back up is with the correct kind of sealant. Loctite 545 is the standard. However, if you have to, go with Teflon tape. Always remember to wrap it tight and in the direction of the threads so that the tape doesn't come right off as the fittings are tightened.

Other Specialty Parts

Every setup is unique, and yours may fall into this category. For example, if you have an engine-driven compressor, then you'll want a spare belt and whatever tools you need to adjust the tensioner. If you have hard lines on your truck, then you may want some soft line and appropriate fittings if something should happen. Just think about the things that are unique to your vehicle and make sure that you're covered. ◼

the bag, and since they can shift on the horizontal axis, it can be difficult to keep them still. They're best used when both mounting points are connected by some kind of pivot. Otherwise, the bag can shift and eventually tear.

Now, if you want a sleeve-style airbag, things change a little bit. You still want a pivot of some kind because the same basic rules apply. However, the difference now is that these bags are traditionally used with setups that either don't require a ton of lift or just want some additional load handling. For example, you'll find them on the back of pickup trucks when the owner wants to carry or tow larger capacities. But, since they ride so nice, they're also used in installs where lift isn't the priority.

Again, most scenarios where you want an airbag have some kind of pivot involved, or even an exist-ing suspension. However, the airbag itself doesn't have any internal support, so if you put it in place where the bag has to support something by itself, it will tear and fail.

Here's a good example: When airbags began to surge in popularity in the 1990s, truck guys were always the ones installing cool setups. However, car enthusiasts (particularly those with the then-ubiquitous Honda Civic or Accord) wanted to do the same thing. They soon learned that it wasn't easy.

An early-1990s Honda Civic or Accord has independent front suspension with a strut that carries the load. The idea back then was to create some kind of platform for the airbag where it replaced the strut entirely. There was now no ride dampening. Instead, the bag would just carry the load. Easy, right?

It turns out that it just didn't work. When inflated, the airbag couldn't keep steady, and either the base or the top would shift, which caused it to go way out of alignment, frequently tearing the airbag in the process.

Today, there's a solution. You can buy strut bags in either sleeve or double-convoluted form, and they're specifically made for those applications. They have a sleeve on the inside of the bag that accepts a strut, sealing them up tight in the process. Now, the strut holds the lateral stress on the suspension just like it does from the factory, and the airbag does the lifting.

The point is that not everything can be put on airbags. That shouldn't stifle you from getting creative—far from it. Instead, get out there and figure out the engineering to do the job right.

Here are two sizes of a traditional double-convoluted airbag. Each one provides different lifting capacities and ride quality. Find the size that both fits in your vehicle and functions the way you want.

This is a sleeve-style airbag made by Slam Specialties. The capacities on this kind of unit aren't as high as on a double-convoluted bag, but they work great in certain scenarios.

Air Systems 101

Up to this point, the discussion has been about the "why" of air-bagged suspensions and how that could fit into your next build. However, it's time to talk about the "how" of the whole thing. How do you airbag your truck, car, or whatever, and how does the process work?

Let's begin with a quick walk-through of how an air system works. This is the nuts and bolts of the whole thing from a 50,000-foot view. The specifics and details are explained later, but for now, it's all about the basics.

The air system itself is made up of several components: the tank, valves, air lines, compressors, pressure switch, switches, and airbags. Each item has its own job. The tank stores the air used for the system, and the valves direct the air via the air lines to its destination: the airbags. The pressure switch tells the compressors to fill up the air tank when it gets lower than a designated pressure. Finally, the switches trigger the opening and closing of the valves.

It sounds pretty simple, and it ultimately is. However, as is to be expected, there's a little bit more to the equation once you get into it.

This 1959 Impala has a compact air setup. That tank is an AccuAir CVT, which has the compressor, tank, and valves all in one unit. (Photo Courtesy Switch Suspension)

Air setups come in all shapes and sizes. This 1967 Cadillac Coupe DeVille has two Viair compressors, an AccuAir eLevel and VU4 manifold, and a seamless air tank. (Photo Courtesy Switch Suspension)

The tank may not just be singular, for example. You can have one large tank, one small one, or multiple tanks to make up one overall size. You can run individual valves that direct the pressure or buy a valve manifold, which is essentially multiple valves with one body. Then, there's digital air management systems, and that's complex enough that it deserves its own chapter, but that is all coming up.

You need to know and understand the fundamentals. For example, if you find that your compressors are

Airbags and Speed

One aspect to consider is speed. Some people want an airbag setup that will literally hop their ride off the ground, while others just want to cruise their car or truck and could care less about how fast it raises or lowers. There's no real wrong answer here; it's all a matter of opinion.

The speed of your setup is based on the smallest-diameter connection in your system. If you have 1/2-inch air lines with 1/4-inch valves, the valves are your bottleneck. Pair each of the connections together so they work in harmony, not opposition.

The general rule for speed is the larger the lines (and connecting fittings and valves), the faster you'll go. It's not unheard of for competition airbag hoppers to run 1-inch lines and larger. Conversely, the smaller you go, the slower you'll lift and/or lower.

Today, speed isn't much of an issue or a priority for most folks, and that's thanks to the rise (pun unintended) of leveling systems.

The problem that's plagued all adjustable suspension systems over the years is the lack of a consistent and reliable height-setting system. If a car or truck was on airbags back in the late 1990s, you would tap or push a switch to lift and lower your vehicle. With both systems, it didn't matter how precisely you made that contact, the results were never the same.

Why? Weight, mostly. If you lifted your vehicle while you were inside, it would naturally raise less on your side. If you had passengers, the same principle applied. Lifting your ride while standing outside of it didn't help, either. After all, once you got in, the whole thing would lean to one side. Pressure gauges didn't help. Thanks to varying barometric pressure and fluctuations in your own weight, it was impossible to dial it in perfectly. Let's just say that somehow you did figure out a perfect system. The moment that you hit a bump or started driving down the road, something would change, and you'd be out of level again. This was a major annoyance, and everyone with adjustable suspension dealt with it.

So, when digital air management systems became popular and, more importantly, reliable, people stopped caring about how fast or slow their airbags lifted. Instead, it just became about fine tuning the speed so things would lift and lower evenly and smoothly. Some put smaller lines in the front and larger in the back because gravity and weight dictate that the front always moves down faster, while the back lifts faster. Others just ran smaller lines overall, including down to 1/4-inch lines, which is something that would've been laughed out of the scene in 2000.

The industry standard now seems to have settled on 3/8-inch-diameter lines, which is both fast enough for the average person and slow enough for a quality leveling system, but there are plenty of 1/4-inch setups out there too. ∎

The air lines coming out of this airbag aren't very large, but they don't have to be. With the right levelling system, everything can still function smoothly. (Photo Courtesy Switch Suspension)

constantly running, you may want to add another tank to your system or upsize your existing model. You'll need to learn how to fix a leak and how to replace an air line if it has an issue.

So, let's dive into the specifics.

Air System Walkthrough

At this point, you know what an airbag is and how the setup works as a whole. However, before you really dive in deep, let's walk through the system itself and how it works.

There are two basic items to think about with an air system setup: how air gets into the tank and how air gets out. Let's start with the tank.

Getting Air into the Tank

The tank is where all of your air is stored. It's what goes out into your airbags too. But how does air get in?

That's the job of the compressor. Just like the compressor in your garage that powers your air tools, this compressor does the same thing.

To build up pressure, the compressor needs a check valve between itself and the tank. A check valve is a one-way valve that's totally passive; it requires no electrical connection to work. These valves have arrows on them that indicate their direction of flow, and without them, the compressor wouldn't be able to build up air.

Now, if it was just a compressor putting out air, then you'd have to manually turn it on and off. But that's annoying, right? Nevermind how unsafe it could be. No, the job of turning the compressor on and off is handled by a pressure switch. This is also plumbed into the tank, and they're sold with different pressure ratings. Basically, just like the name

sounds, it detects how much pressure is in the tank. If it's lower than its rated pressure, the switch is on and the compressor(s) will run. However, if the rated pressure is reached, the pressure switch turns off, and so does the compressor. (The wiring and specifics of the pressure switch are discussed in Chapter 3.)

This system puts air into the tank: 1) The pressure switch determines if air is needed in the tank or not. a) If yes, it turns on, triggering the compressor. b) If no, it turns off, cutting off power to the compressor. 2) The compressor puts air into the tank.

Easy, right?

Getting Air Out of the Tank

To get air into the tank, you need check valves that allow the air to flow just one way: in. Anything else that's connected to the tank that

This is a basic corner setup featuring two valves. In this case, the T-fitting in the middle is mounted to the airbag via a swivel fitting. The valve on the right accepts air from the tank (the fitting on the right), delivering it into the airbag, and the left valve dumps the air out of the bag.

If you follow the Viair compressor's leader hose to the right, there's a large black fitting going into the tank. That's the check valve, and without it, the compressor wouldn't be able to build up any pressure. (Photo Courtesy Switch Suspension)

doesn't have some kind of valve or directional device will fill up when the tank fills up. Therefore, if you were only to connect the airbags directly to the tank, every time the compressor turned on, the airbags would fill until the pressure in the entire system hit the PSI the pressure switch dictated—and that wouldn't be a great way to roll.

The solution, just like you have with the compressor, is a directional device to tell the air when to stop and when to go. It's a switch made for air, and in the case of an air suspension system, it's called a valve.

The type of valve used for airbags is basically an electrically controlled check valve. In the case of most air systems, they're set up to be closed when there's no power applied to them. Once they're powered on, the valve opens, sending air to whatever it's plumbed to. It's usually an airbag, but it can be two airbags if you want. It's totally up to you. (Chapter 5 contains more information about valves.)

However, that only puts air *into* the airbag. How do you get it out? Unfortunately, you can't just open that valve again and put the air back into the tank. Instead, you need a second valve. This one is mounted so that it's after the first valve and after the airbag. Often, you'll see two valves connected with a T-fitting with the base of the T running to the airbag. Therefore, if you want to inflate the airbag, you open Valve 1. When you want to deflate the airbag, you open Valve 2. At that point, the system is back to where it started.

Basic Air System

Let's walk through that scenario in illustration form. This is for a simple, four-airbag setup with two

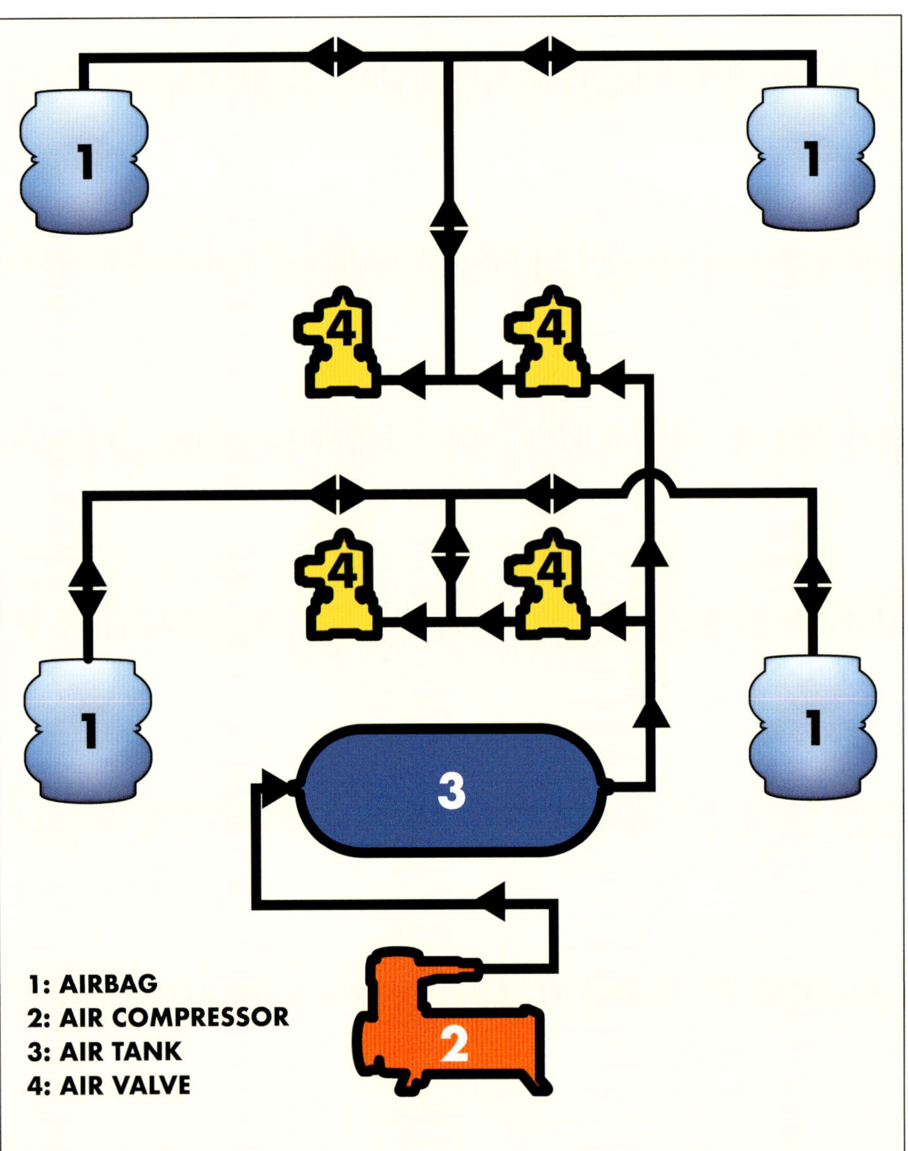

This basic diagram illustrates how an airbag system works. In this case, there are four airbags (one per corner) and four valves. Here the bags are tee'd together via the valves, which allows air to transfer between the pair.

valves: one for the front and one for the rear. Let's begin by focusing first on the airflow.

In the diagram above, there are a few things to note. There are four airbags (all labeled with a "1") that each represent a corner of the vehicle. At the bottom, there is an air compressor (labeled with a "2"), and right above it, the air tank (labeled with a "3"). Above that are four valves (each one is labeled with a "4").

The line in the diagram represents the air path, and arrows show the direction of flow. For example, coming from the air compressor and going to the tank, the air can only flow one way: into the tank. However, the airbags have arrows going both ways. That's because air comes in and leaves the airbags through the valves.

How does that work? Well, if you follow the line from the right side of

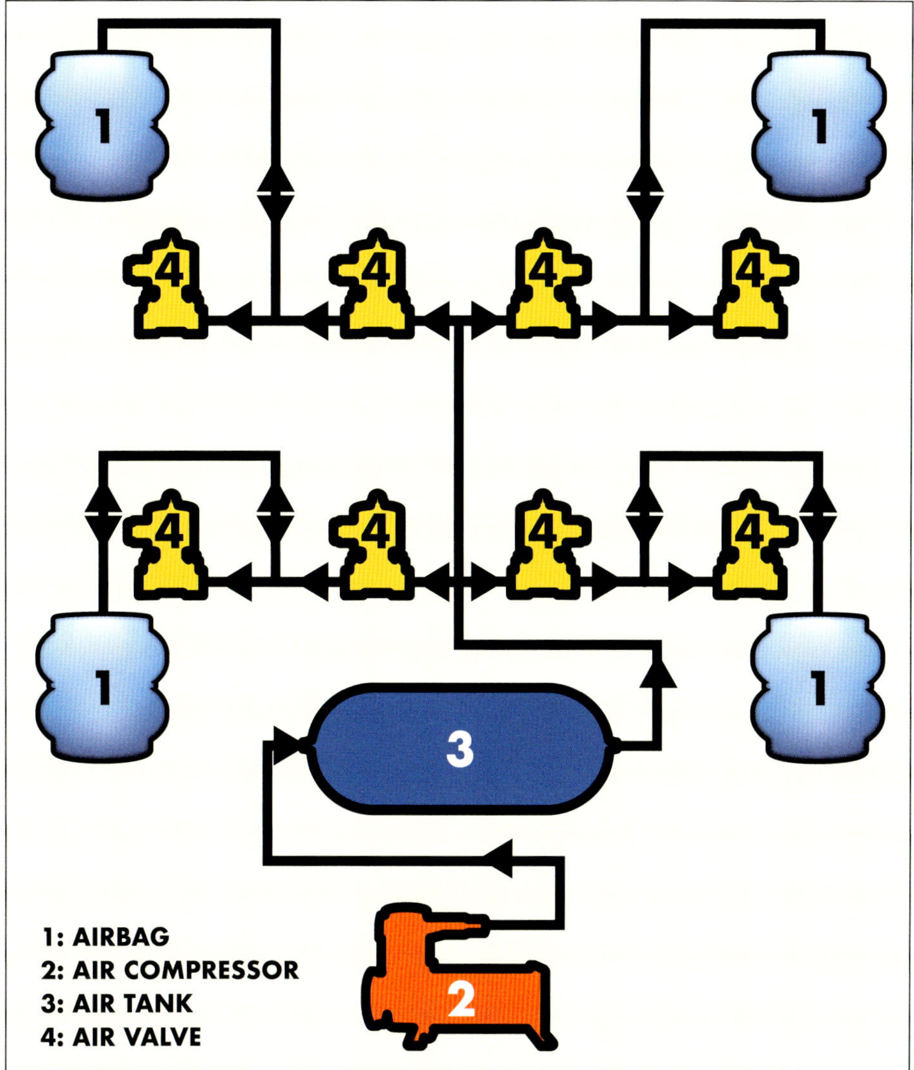

The standard air system, like the basic system, has four airbags. But now there are eight valves, which means there's a pair per corner. This isolates the airbags from any air transfer and provides the most adjustability for this type of setup.

the tank, it goes up, Ts off into the bottom pair of valves, and then goes into the top pair. Each valve grouping in this scenario runs to a pair of airbags; one goes to the front, and one goes to the rear. The arrows show how it flows.

Look at the bottom pair of valves. First, the air flows into the valve on the right. Then, it exits that valve, and fills up the valve to the left and the airbags. The air valve on the right acts as a check valve for the air; the airbags have pressure in them, and air cannot leave until the valve on the left opens. When it does, the air releases out of that system and goes into the atmosphere.

Now, this is a very basic valve setup and one that some people use when they're starting out. It has some drawbacks.

Look at the top pair of airbags and notice how the air flows. The air line forms a "T" and branches off to each bag. So, the two airbags are tied together with the lines. This matters because now every time you turn, the weight of the vehicle transfers, and when it does, the air shifts to the opposite side. It's definitely not optimal. Some of this movement can be lessened with sway bars, but it doesn't go away entirely. If you can avoid it, try not to use this system on your vehicle.

Standard Air System

Let's take it up a notch and show one of the common setups you'll find: a four-corner airbag setup with eight valves.

Now, this is the kind of setup that is found in many vehicles (particularly in the early 2000s) prior to the rise in popularity of the manifold. The difference is that the number of valves has doubled. Now, there's a pair of valves for each airbag: one lift and one drop (or dump, to use hydraulic parlance).

Let's walk through the basics of this setup. Again, the air compressor feeds air to the tank. A line (or "lines" in the real world) from the tank feeds each valve pairing. Each corner now has its own valve setup and is no longer tied to another corner. That makes this an optimal system for tweaking and tuning the handling as well as providing flexibility with adjusting the individual corners.

This system is great for all the reasons listed above, but on the downside, it can get pricey. A lot of fittings are required to connect all of those valves, and that is not an inexpensive process. Plus, every connection is a potential leak.

So yes, a standard air system works, and it's definitely an option for the average builder. However, if you want to step it up a notch, it's time to look at the next choice.

This is a typical air valve assembly circa 2005. The T-fitting in the middle sends air from the tank to each valve assembly. Obviously, a downside is the space that the valves occupy, particularly when you need one more of these too.

Manifold Air System

Today, the system that most people use is a valve manifold. It's a simple, easy, and clean way to control your airbags, and they have a lot of advantages.

Things get more complicated, yet somehow simpler with an air manifold. These are machined blocks (typically made of aluminum) that house multiple valves in one body. This means that both the lift and drop valves are in one spot, and the overall space requirements are reduced by at least a quarter. That, and they look much better.

Note in the diagram how all four airbags run into one manifold. Now, think about how that would work on your project. Just mount the valve manifold in one spot, and all the lines run to it. That makes for a faster and more tidy install too.

The downside is that they're expensive. When they are compared to the cost of valves and the fittings that are required to connect everything, it doesn't quite even out, but it's not as bad as you may think.

Four- and eight-valve manifolds are available that will run two and four corners, respectively.

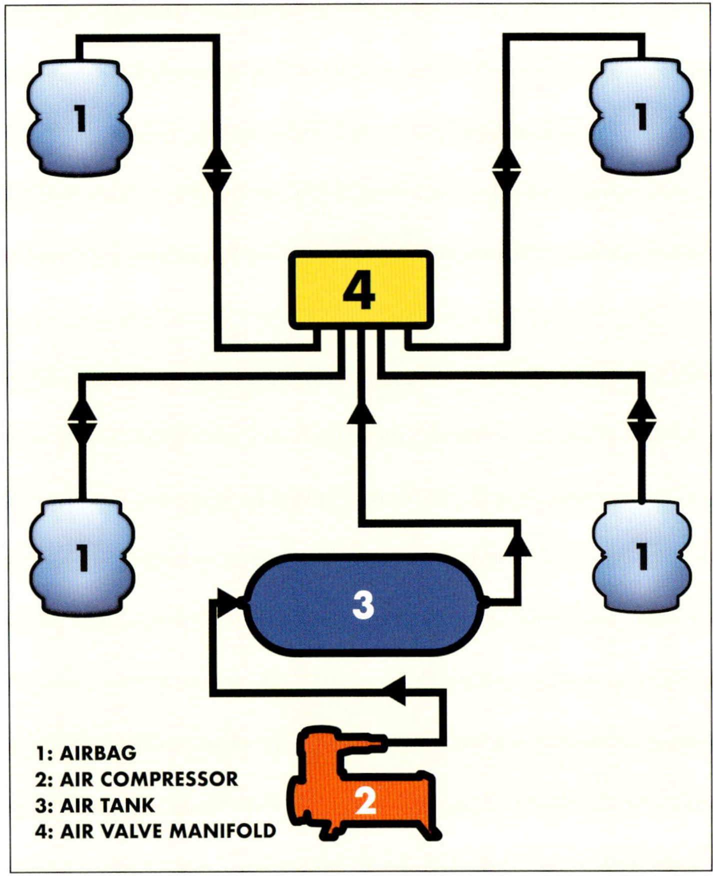

This is an AccuAir VU4 manifold. Notice how all four air lines run out of the bottom of the assembly, which makes it a cleaner install overall. (Photo Courtesy Switch Suspension)

This air system uses a valve manifold. It takes the eight valves that are in the standard system and puts them into one container, which makes wiring and plumbing easier and more compact.

COMPRESSORS

If you want a reliable, functional air suspension, then you need at least one reliable, functional air compressor. It's the heart of your system, and it needs to work flawlessly. Otherwise, when you're lifting and lowering your ride, you risk running out of air.

However, there's a lot to know about how these things work before you dive right in. What is a duty cycle? What is CFM? What combination of those do you need to get the right compressor(s) for your setup?

Let's talk about it. But first, it's time to talk about the basics.

Definition and Function

An air compressor is built to generate air and deliver it into a storage unit of some kind, usually a tank. Once the tank reaches the pressure that is designated by the pressure switch (more on that later), it turns off. That's pretty much the gist.

When it comes to air suspension systems, they're what replenishes your supply. Think of it like having a gas station in the trunk of your car. Whenever you need fuel—in this case, air—it's there at the flip of a switch or it comes on automatically whenever the air runs low.

There are a few things that you need to know first, and they deal with how the compressor is rated. For the purposes of this section, I use the popular Viair 480C compressor as an example.

The first term is cubic feet per minute (CFM). It deals with how quickly the air compressor can push the air to the storage unit, and it varies based on the amount of pressure that's already in the tank. The Viair 480C is rated at 1.86 cfm. For perspective, that means that if you had an air tank that was 2 feet square, it would fill up in just over 1 minute.

The next term is pounds per square inch (PSI), which is the basic unit of measurement for air in your system. You'll use this for everything: the PSI in your airbags, the PSI in your tank, the PSI rating of your

The compressor on this truck (a Viair 480C) is mounted under the bed and will see water, rain, and dirt. Fortunately, it's a sealed compressor, so that's not a problem.

pressure switch, etc. When it comes to the compressor, you want to know the maximum working pressure it will produce, and in the case of the Viair 480C it's 200 psi.

Why is the PSI rating important? It's because above that point, the compressor doesn't function efficiently, if at all. If you get a compressor that maxes out at 100 psi, lifting anything heavy is going to take time and may even require the compressor to run. However, if your compressor tops out at a higher PSI, you can run higher pressures in the tank without worrying about replenishment.

Another thing to look for is whether or not the compressor is sealed or non-sealed. As the term implies, it has to do with whether the compressor is protected from dust and moisture. This mostly matters if you're exposing your compressor to the elements, such as underneath the bed of a truck. In that case, use a sealed model. Otherwise, the first puddle that you drive through could cause your compressor to fail. The Viair 480C is a sealed compressor, so it can be mounted anywhere.

Always Use a Leader Hose

Whatever compressor you buy, it will more than likely come with a leader hose. This is a stainless-steel line that threads into the top of the compressor and then outputs to an NPT fitting. This is designed to run into your tank, which makes installation easy. Here's the thing: don't ever consider changing that out with another line.

That leader hose serves two purposes. First, it helps dissipate heat. The compressor is going to get hot no matter what you do, and if hot air gets into your tank, it will condense and form water, which is bad (check out more about water traps in Chapter 4). It also contains a check valve, and that's absolutely necessary. Otherwise, your air compressor won't have any way to compress air, and that's a pretty major issue.

Now, some people dispute this idea. They want to mount the compressors somewhere farther away than a leader hose reaches, so they use their own line and a check valve to get the air the distance. As long as you have the supplied stainless-steel leader hose in place, you're fine. However, if you swap it with something else, you may have problems.

Say that you replace the leader hose with a check valve and some D.O.T.-approved soft line. It's almost a guarantee that the line will get a hole in it within the first few minutes of use (and if not, the first week for sure). There's just too much heat. If you use hard line, you're in another bad situation. Compressors use rubber mounting pads because they vibrate a lot. If you secure a hard line in place and then connect that to something else that's also solid mounted, there's no more wiggle room. It may not happen right away, but that metal line will eventually fatigue and break.

In the real world, a hard line can be used between the compressor and tank as long as a check valve is used. In addition, if both the tank and the compressor employ some kind of rubber mount, the movement should be fine. However, know that the manufacturer doesn't recommend it, and there is the potential for problems—even if it's not immediate.

The point is that your compressor should come with a leader hose. Use it, and if it ever fails, replace it with the same model. It's an important part of the air system. ■

The leader hose on this Viair compressor has clearly labelled instructions. Follow them. Otherwise, you could have a leak or a compressor that just doesn't work.

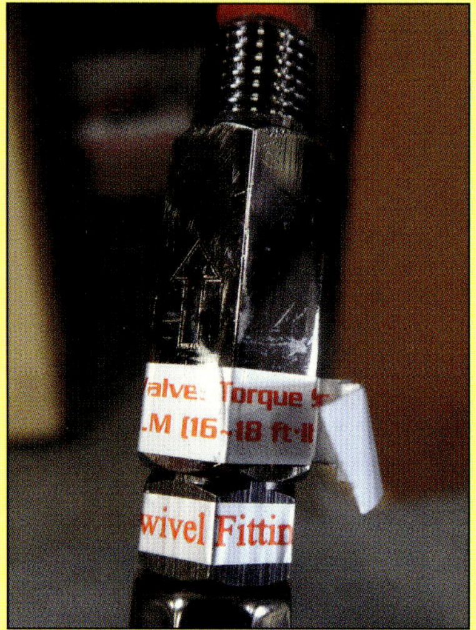

The check valve on the end of the leader hose not only has a direction marked on it but it's also mounted to a swivel fitting. This makes it easier to install. Otherwise, the line would get all twisted up.

This is another Viair compressor but in black. The round piece on the left is the air filter, and if it gets clogged up, clean and/or replace it just like you would on your vehicle's engine.

Then, there's the duty cycle. A compressor functions in two states: running and not running. The duty cycle represents how long the compressor can run within a designated period of time at 100 psi and at 72°F. Viair has a great chart about this on its website, but for perspective, a compressor with a 25-percent duty cycle (designated as one hour, 100 psi at 72°F) will run for 15 minutes and then have to recover for 45 minutes. A 50-percent duty cycle is 30 minutes on, then 30 minutes off, and 100 percent means a full 1-hour run time.

Let's put that into practice. The Viair 480C has a 100-percent duty cycle at 100 psi and 50 percent at 200 psi. That means it can run for an hour solid if you're just trying to get the tank to 100 psi, but at 200 psi, it can only go for 30 minutes. In practice, both of those times are more than enough to lift your vehicle, empty the tank (or come close), and refill, assuming that you're running a reasonable tank size.

Maximum air tank size is another item to consider. When building your setup, try to pair your tank(s) and compressors. Therefore, you should know the maximum air tank size rating for your compressors. With the 480C, it's 5 gallons. So, if you had two 3-gallon tanks, you might want to run two 480Cs to cover the 6 gallons of air in use. If you had one 5-gallon tank, one 480C would be fine. Although, you could do two if you wanted.

Fill rates are also important. You need to know how long it will take to fill your tank from completely empty, to half loaded, and so on. Viair has a chart on its website with specifications for each compressor. The chart below is for the 480C with a 5-gallon gas tank.

Amount	Duration
0–145 psi	6 minutes, 2 seconds
110–145 psi	1 minute 15 seconds
0–200 psi	10 minutes, 30 seconds
165–200 psi	3 minutes, 10 seconds

In the real world, it's rare that you'll need your compressor to fill your tank from empty. So, using the example above, if you have a 145-psi pressure switch, it'll take just over 1 minute to fill your 5-gallon tank. That's not bad at all.

Finally, you need to know the maximum 12-volt amperage draw. You're most likely going to run your compressor(s) off the vehicle's 12-volt battery, and you need a high-voltage relay to go between the pressure switch and the compressor(s). If you know the amperage rating, you can more accurately select what size of relay is needed. The Viair 480C has a max 12-volt amperage draw of 23 amps. You could connect a 40-amp relay for that compressor and be fine, or, if you're running two compressors, a 60- or 80-amp relay. Many aftermarket suppliers offer single- and dual-compressor wiring kits that include the appropriate relays.

Compressor Selection

Now you know the ins and outs of compressors, but how do you use that information to figure out which compressor you need and if you need more than one? Let's figure it out.

Start with what you want out of your setup. You probably fall into one of two categories: 1) you want to adjust your ride height frequently, or 2) you just want to get in and go.

People in the first category need more storage (tanks) and, therefore, more compressors. That's because you'll be putting a lot of demands on the system, and if you're constantly refilling the airbags, you'll need air to put into them. For someone in that category, consider at least two tanks and at least two compressors.

If you're in the second category, you can make due with much less. Most digital air management systems don't require as much air, as they're only called upon once the ride is started up and parked. Although they frequently make minor adjustments up and down, the compressor isn't called into duty that often. Therefore, you can run just one tank and compressor if you like. Although, most people still feel better running

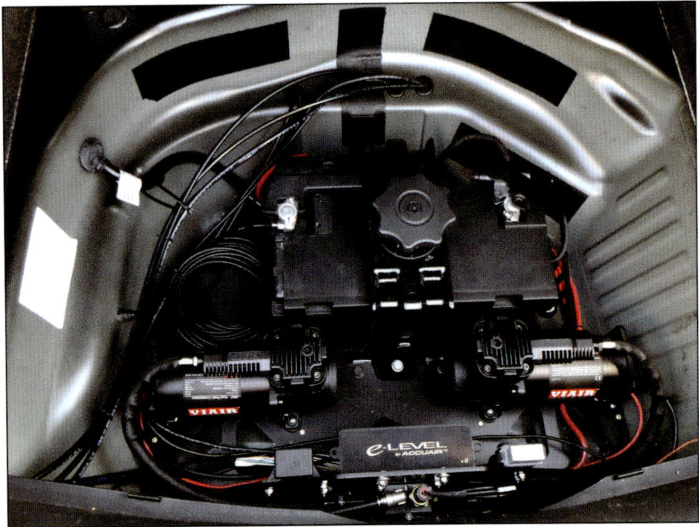

This 2010 Audi A4 runs a pair of Viair compressors hidden under the trunk floor right next to the battery. The tank is visible when you open the rear decklid. (Photo Courtesy Switch Suspension)

Many truck builders build compressor mounts into the frame so that they're out of the way. Use sealed compressors when doing that. Otherwise, you risk them failing.

more just in case a compressor fails or for extra refill speed.

The next consideration is the mounting location. Truck builders often install the compressors either under the bed or in it. However, in both scenarios, the compressor is exposed to the elements (assuming there's not a cover over and under the air system). Those scenarios require a sealed compressor. Car builders, on the other hand, frequently put the compressor(s) in the trunk, and that's relatively dust- and moisture-free. In that situation, a sealed or non-sealed compressor can be used. With that being said, sealed will always be better than a non-sealed compressor, simply because the risk of damage from dust and debris is removed.

Realistically, you're probably only going to find sealed compressors on the market. However, there are non-sealed units out there. If you have the choice, go with sealed.

What's next? Go back to the mounting location and think about how you want to mount the compressors: vertically in their standard orientation, on their sides, or even upside down? That decision will change what compressor you select.

Earlier in this chapter I wrote about the Viair 480C, which is a sealed compressor. It's also one that doesn't require oil, and that's important for certain mounting situations. If you want to put the compressor on its side or upside down, it must be oil-free. Otherwise, it won't lubricate the piston properly and will burn out sooner.

With all that said, you can narrow down your options even further by choosing between the three major types of compressors: electric, engine driven, and hybrid.

Electric Compressors

These are, by far, the most common type of compressor. From Accu-Air to Viair to Ridetech, there are many companies that sell and manufacture electric air compressors, all of varying quality. You already know about sealed versus non-sealed, but what else do you need to know about electric compressors?

Electric compressors require electricity, naturally, so they need a reliable 12-volt source. Most of the time, the stock alternator on a vehicle will work well, so there's no need to upgrade. However, if you use more than two compressors, you might consider getting a higher-amperage alternator to keep up with the demand.

Also, think about getting a better battery or possibly two or more. Most people with airbagged suspensions use a deep-cycle battery that can handle multiple draining sessions reliably. Optima and Odyssey are two companies that make deep-cycle batteries, and they're both gel cells, which is also a nice feature because you don't have to worry about refilling or maintaining them. You can also mount a gel-cell battery in different orientations, which is good if you want to mount the batteries closer to the air management setup.

If you have multiple compressors, consider multiple batteries so that you always have enough power storage to get things up and moving.

This Viair compressor is mounted upside down in the trunk of a 1977 Malibu. Note that it's wired directly into a 40-amp relay. (Photo Courtesy Switch Suspension)

The part just forward of the brake master cylinder is an engine-driven compressor, and it provides a huge boost in CFM.

Of course, that also might necessitate a larger alternator depending on your vehicle, so consider that as well.

Every kind of compressor needs a switch of some sort to trigger it, and in the case of most electric compressors, that's a pressure switch. There are more details about them later in this chapter, but the idea is that the compressors only turn on when the pressure in the tank dips below a preset amount. It's a convenient way to keep things running smoothly without having to manually turn them on and off.

Engine-Driven Compressors

If you want a system that's always ready to go, consider an engine-driven compressor. These are units that mount to the front of the engine block and create compressed air using an accessory pulley. Many times, these are recycled and repurposed air-conditioner compressors, and they work great. Not only are they fast but they're also easy to use.

Engine-driven compressors are not perfect, however. First, they're big. In addition, for many people, they're an eyesore in the engine bay since they tend to stick outside of the normal spot where you'd find an engine accessory, and they're just generally awkward.

They can be finicky too. Since these are often used with recycled or rebuilt parts, they can wear out, and when they do, you're stuck. If you don't own a vehicle with a GM V-8, you might have to fabricate the kit yourself; it seems like most kits are made for full-size trucks and cars, most of them being Chevys. Oh, and there's the maintenance too. They need to be oiled, and that oil must be changed regularly, which can be a bit of a pain.

The benefits, though, are pretty great. Watching the gauge on your tank pressure rocket up is quite satisfying, and you also don't have to stress about wiring anything heavy-duty because the compressor is triggered by a 14-gauge lead.

If only there was some kind of combination device . . .

Hybrid Compressors

Admittedly, there aren't many of these available, and they tend to be found more in the 4x4 world.

However, if you want an electric, engine-driven compressor, check out Oasis Manufacturing.

Oasis took an engine-driven compressor and mounted a 5-hp electric motor to it to create a hybrid of the two styles. They're heavy-duty deals that have a 100-percent duty cycle at 200 psi. However, they also can require up to 180 amps to run, which is no small amount, considering that the Viair 480C takes 23. They're also not quiet, so putting them in the trunk of your car is probably not a great idea.

Oasis compressors were a lot more popular in the airbag world prior to automatic levelling systems. Back then, people wanted their bags fast, and to do that, a nitrogen tank and larger air lines were needed or a compressor that could handle the load. Oasis could do that and power your air tools, so they seemed like the logical choice.

Today, the tendency is to lean more toward slower, more-reliable setups that don't have such immense air movement. But if you want the speed and don't have an engine that can easily support an engine-driven

The Oasis compressor pictured in the top-left corner of the bed is a good example of a hybrid compressor.

compressor, a hybrid might be your best choice.

Pressure Switches

There has been a lot of talk so far in this chapter about pressure switches and a lot of teasing about how more details are yet to come. Guess what? They're here.

A pressure switch tells the compressors when to turn on and off based on the pressure in the tank. If the pressure dips below the rated "on pressure" on your pressure switch, it will turn on, and it will run until it reaches the rated "off pressure." This ensures that the tank(s) will always sit somewhere between the on and off pressure ratings on your pressure switch.

As such, when you're shopping for pressure switches, you'll find them with an "on/off" number. For example, Viair lists a few different sizes:

On Pressure	Off Pressure
85 psi	105 psi
90 psi	120 psi
110 psi	145 psi
145 psi	175 psi
165 psi	200 psi

That brings up another question: which pressure switch size do you need? Well, it depends on what you want.

The lower the overall pressure in your tank, the quicker you'll run out of air—that's the first consideration. Second, if your car or truck is pretty heavy, it'll need a certain amount of pressure to lift it up. Third, what's the maximum PSI rating in your tank? It matters because you certainly don't want to exceed that. Finally, what's the duty cycle and max working pressure of your compressor? All of these things have to be factored in properly for you to determine what size you need.

With all that said, start with an "on PSI" rating of at least 100 psi if you're lifting any kind of roadworthy vehicle (for example, a Honda Accord as opposed to a golf cart). You'll want at least 100 psi to lift the weight. Then, start considering the max PSI in your tank. Lots of people run a "145 on/175 off" pressure switch, but if the tank has more headroom, the "165/200" isn't bad, either. Then, look at the duty cycle of the compressor as well as the max working pressure. If the

This is a Viair pressure switch, and it's a "165 on/200 off" model. This one is pretty popular because many people want to run higher pressures in their system.

max working pressure is less than 200 psi a 200-psi pressure switch will leave your compressor running all day long. However, if the max working pressure was 220 or 250 psi, you'd be just fine.

So, initially, this seems like a lot of back and forth to figure out what works and what doesn't. However, in reality, it's not that bad. Just look at the work pressure of your compressor(s), the maximum pressure in your tank(s), and the weight of your vehicle. If you need a starting point, go with a "145/175" and see how it works. You can always go up or down from there.

Wiring a Pressure Switch

Now you know what a pressure switch is and how it works, but how does that get power to the compressor? That's easy: with a relay.

There are two types of relays that can be used, and they're based on the amount of amperage they can handle. Many compressors operate on an under-30-amp load, so you can use a 30/40-amp Bosch relay to handle a single compressor. If you're running more

The object with the plastic cap on the left side of the T-fitting is a pressure switch. Always plumb it into the tank itself (on the other side of the tee is an air fitting to run to a tank pressure gauge).

than one compressor, you can either connect the power and pressure switch wiring from one relay to the next or run a heavy-duty relay, which is typically around 80 amps.

Once you add more compressors, things get a bit more complex. You can either add more relays per compressor, or just get a larger, more heavy-duty relay to handle the load. If you're running multiple compressors, having a larger one not only tends to be more reliable but also more convenient during installation.

Another issue is how you wire things up. The compressors should be run right to the battery via the relay. That way, they get strong current with a larger cable. The pressure switch will need power too, and it only requires a 12- to 14-gauge lead. Do you connect that straight to the battery or to a wire that only turns on when the ignition is on?

This is up to you, but it comes with a few caveats. The safest way is to run it to the ignition lead, and there are a few reasons why. Say that the tank develops a leak, and overnight it empties out all of its air. If your pressure switch is wired to the ignition lead, you're fine; your battery will be at normal charge levels. Sure, you'll have to wait for your tank to fill up, but your car or truck will start, and that's the important part.

This is a standard Bosch-style relay. Each pole has a different number and purpose, and they act like a power-triggered switch.

To use a relay to connect a pressure switch and compressor, wire the 87 pole to the positive lead on the compressor; 85 to ground; 86 to the pressure switch; and 30 to a 12-volt source, such as the battery.

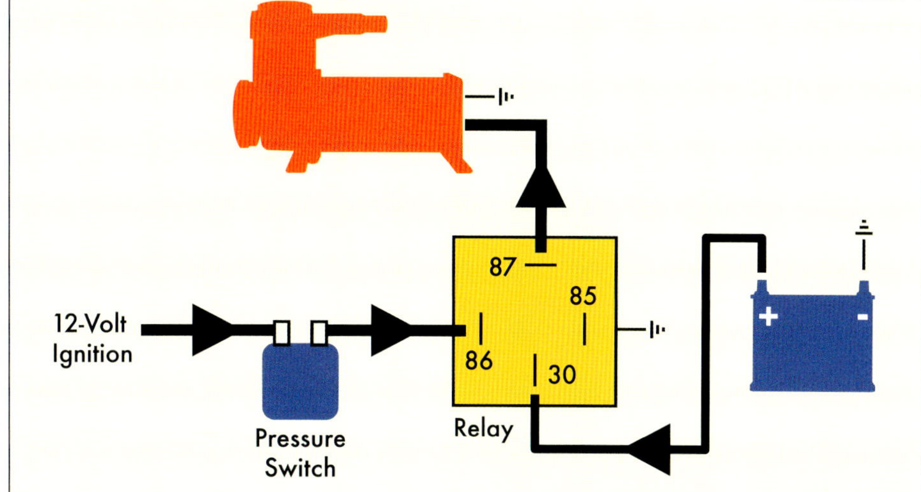

This simple diagram shows how to use a standard 12-volt relay to trigger the compressor.

If you go with constant power in that same scenario, the compressors will kick on and off all night, which will likely drain the battery. If you're in a garage, that might not be a big deal. However, if you're parked at an airport overnight or just away from your ride, that could be a bigger issue. Worse yet, what if a relay fails, causing it to push power constantly to the compressors? You could end up with an electrical fire or an exploded tank, neither of which are good for you, your vehicle, or your health.

The best option then is to power it via the ignition lead, but there is one other choice. You can also wire it to a manual switch. In this scenario, if you want to leave the switch on overnight you can. It's up to you. It also gives you the flexibility to turn the compressors off while you're driving for whatever reason.

This is a heavy-duty 80-amp relay wired for use with two Viair 480C compressors. The threaded posts make it easier to use with ring terminals, which is a better option than going with smaller relays and spade connectors.

The choice is yours. Just know your options and their potential consequences.

TANKS, FITTINGS, AND AIR LINES

An air suspension setup requires many components, and it's easy to give some of them more or less thought than others. After all, you'll probably sweat the details when it comes time to pick a compressor, but what fittings do you need? Who cares, right?

Well, you should care. Although these are the types of things that are often overlooked, they're critical to your setup. Without the right fittings, you'll have reliability issues. Without the right tank (or tanks), you'll run out of air frequently or find your compressor(s) running constantly trying to fill them. Also, the right air line makes the difference between finding yourself on the side of the road and not.

This is important stuff, so take the time to do it right.

Tanks

Pop the trunk or look at the chassis on any airbagged vehicle, and you'll find an air tank of some kind. Sometimes it's an oval tube, other times it's the frame itself. Some method for holding air in the system is needed. Otherwise, you won't be able to lift the vehicle.

Two air tanks sit in the bed of this Ford F-150, and they're enough to get the job done.

Airbags take pressure to inflate, and you can't get that from a compressor pushing air by itself. The air needs to be compressed, and the only way to do that is through some method of storage. That's your air tank.

Think of it like your car's battery. Sitting there by itself, it has 12 to 14 volts of power ready to use. When you turn the key (or push the button on your fancy newer ride), the starter motor draws power from the battery, draining it in the process. As you drive, other systems demand electrical power, and they call upon the battery to keep them running. What fills the battery back up? The alternator. It's constantly generating the power that the battery needs, and the cycle continues.

If the analogy is taken further, the battery is like an air tank and the alternator is like an air compressor.

The compressor fills the tank, and the tank is constantly called upon for air.

Now, the tricky part when selecting a tank is figuring out how much capacity you need. Tanks are typically measured in gallons (1, 3, 5, etc.), and since they come in many shapes and dimensions, you have many options. How do you know what the right size is for you? Good question. Let's find out.

Tank Selection

The first item to consider is the size and weight of your vehicle. If you're putting airbags on a 1995 Honda Civic, you're not dealing with a lot of weight. It won't take a lot of pressure to inflate those bags, either. However, if you have a crew cab Ford F-350 dually and you plan on using it to tow, then there are other concerns. Will you have enough capacity? Do you want to run air tools off the system? What are your needs?

Those are a lot of questions to answer, but fortunately, you have options. Tanks come in a wide variety of sizes, so when in doubt, start small and expand later. Begin with a 3- or 5-gallon tank and then add another if necessary. All you need to do is run a new line to connect the two, and you're golden.

It brings up another obvious question: where do you put the air tank(s)? That's another aspect that factors into the size decision. On most passenger cars, the obvious spot is the trunk. You can usually put a 5-gallon tank mounted parallel to the axles in the back and then have room for compressors on the sides. Otherwise, if you want to remove the spare tire, you can sometimes get a 3-gallon tank in there depending on the available space.

In this situation, two identical tanks were combined with a 1/2-inch straight-pipe nipple, which effectively doubled the overall storage. Not all tanks are built alike, so consider using tubing and PTC fittings if necessary.

Trucks and body-on-frame cars have a whole other series of options. With trucks, the obvious location is the bed. However, because many people build their trucks with the bed off, they end up putting the tank(s) either in the spot for the original spare tire or somewhere else on the frame. Creative locations include the side of the frame under the cab, or way back by the bumper. If your truck's bodystyle came with optional dual gas tanks but is only equipped with one, put a tank or two in the remaining spot. There are many options.

Unibody cars are different. They don't have the same kind of frame to work with, so often you're left with putting the tank(s) either in the trunk or making modifications to the body so the tank(s) can sit underneath. For example, some people take out their spare tire and put their air tank in that void, while others cut out the factory spare tire well entirely, weld in a plate, and then bolt the tanks to the underside of the car in that spot. Again, it's up to you.

You have to think about the quantity of tanks you want and where you could put them. Then, decide what works with your budget and go from there. A good starting point is a single 5-gallon tank, but remember, you can always add more later. That's one of the benefits to airbags, so don't forget about it.

There's one other item to consider, and that's the length of your air line runs. The line that goes from the valve to the tank is additional

The tanks used in this setup had optional mounts to weld in place. These allow you to bolt the tanks in and remove them just as easily if necessary.

volume that you'll have to fill every time you hit the switch. If you have a Ford Focus, that's no big deal. However, put that on a crew cab Dodge dually, and you could have an additional 20 feet to work with. If you have any concerns, you can always add another tank.

Ports and Locations

Another thing to think about with your tank choice is the amount and size of the ports. There is more information about this later in this book, but the speed of your system is limited by the smallest port. So, if you want to lift the vehicle fast, 1/2-inch lines and valves make a lot of sense. However, if you have the valves connected to the tank with 1/4-inch lines, you're putting a kink in the system. If anything, you want to go in reverse: bigger ports on the tank and smaller on the valves. Then, you'll never choke anything out.

Also, consider the number of ports. If you're running a valve manifold, you need one line to fill it that runs from the tank. You'll also have a pressure switch, drain port, and at least one compressor that goes in the tank as well, which gives you a minimum of four ports. If you're doing individual valves located closer to the airbags, you have another four ports to add on. More compressors add to the list as well.

Then, there's *where* those ports are located. There can be a drain port, and it should be on the bottom to let gravity work. The rest of the fittings and their placement comes down to where you put the remainder of the system. Some people like to hide their air lines. If they mount the tank in the trunk of a car, they put the lines so that they run toward the front and therefore away from the viewer. Other people run ornate hard lines, and they put their ports on the opposite side to show off their work. It comes down to personal preference and your particular set-up's requirements.

Tank Material

Consider what the tank is made from. It seems like a silly detail, but it's pretty important in the grand scheme of things mainly because of water.

As previously mentioned, moisture builds up during the air-compression process, and it will sit in the bottom of the tank. Some tanks (typically cheaply made ones) are built with steel, and steel rusts. Better ones are aluminum, but since aluminum is a softer metal than some of the fittings, you could strip out the tank. Then, there's stainless steel, which is also rustproof and, like aluminum, can polish up nicely.

Realistically, it takes years for the inside of a steel air tank to rust. However, since these are one of those "set it and forget it" type of things, it's best to start with a firm foundation.

Another relatively new option is a tank that uses composite materials. For example, The Original Square-Tank has a composite tank that is flanked by two billet aluminum end caps. If you're looking for something that won't rust and will stand out in a crowd, consider something similar that's made with a different type of material entirely.

Water Traps

There's one other aspect to consider with the overall tank setup: a water trap. If you live in an area with lots of humidity or where the temperature dips into the freezing range, consider getting one.

A water trap, well, traps water. It seems obvious, and you've probably seen them in commercial air

Draining Your Tank

An aspect that a lot of people don't consider is that their air tank will build up moisture internally. Since most tanks are made from steel or some variation, over time, that condensation causes it to rot from the inside out, eventually forming leaks. That's when you need to replace the tank entirely.

The fix is to regularly drain the tank. You can do that with something as simple as a draincock mounted to the bottom. Just open it up, let the air pressure push the water out, and you're good.

The problem is that some people have their tanks inside their trunks, and rusty water can make a mess. In that case, an option is to run a single valve right off the bottom of the tank. Take an air line, route it outside the trunk, and then connect it to the valve. When you want to empty the tank, just trigger the valve, and it'll release the air outside of the vehicle. No more mess.

Yes, there's the added cost of adding a valve to your system and the time it takes to wire it. However, in the end, you'll remove the friction point that usually comes with draining a tank (for example, crawling under the car and opening a ball valve) and make it easy. That alone is worth it. ■

This is The Original SquareTank, and it has a composite center portion. It's sandwiched by two aluminum end caps that have NPT ports built in. (Photo Courtesy Switch Suspension)

compressor situations. They're not very common with modern airbag setups though, and that's because they're not strictly necessary. Just like a traditional water trap on the air compressor you may have in your shop or garage, it stops water from getting to the object you have plugged in at the end of the line. In this case, it'll be your valves and airbags.

If you don't run a water trap, you risk having problems, particularly if you're in one of those previously mentioned humid or cold climates. Valves can stick over time by getting gunked up with corrosion, as can your fittings (assuming they're steel). Basically, a water trap is another line of defense in the whole process.

So, where do you put one? Well, it depends on how your setup is designed. Ideally, it goes between the line from your tank to the valves. However, you may have four banks of valves, and that would necessitate four water traps, which seems like overkill. If you're running a manifold, you'll have one feed line for sure, and that could hold your water trap.

Another item to note: keep the water trap low if possible. Gravity causes water to run to the lowest point, so having it down there will help.

Compressed Gas

If you want to build a hopper (a vehicle designed to launch the front or rear tires off the ground with the power of the airbags), you need to get as much pressure out of the tank as fast as possible. To do so, consider a compressed gas tank.

You can get a tank filled with a compressed gas (nitrogen being the most popular option) and a pressure regulator to establish how much pressure is in the system. You still have valves and lines, but now everything is usually much bigger and beefier (3/4- and 1-inch hydraulic lines and valves, typically) so that you can accommodate the pressure you're putting into the system. Your airbags have similarly sized ports.

The idea is that you're replacing the "slow" air compressors and tank setup with something that has instant and always-on pressure. Now, that also means that when the tank runs out, you're out of air—and potentially out of luck if you find yourself on the side of the road. The other problem? Well, if you've ever driven on a freeway and seen a truck with a diamond-shaped sign on the back that reads "Compressed Gas," you know that having something like that in your car or truck is dangerous. Getting into an accident could knock off the regulator. That turns the bottle into a missile that's aimed to go

The huge green bottles with the flames are compressed air tanks, and the regulator is shown at the top of the one on the left. Whenever the owner of this truck wants speed, he swaps out a few connections and goes to town.

out (not up), causing serious harm to you, bystanders, and your ride in the process. Photos exist of vehicles that have been the victims of exploded bottles, and they're not pretty.

So, can you do this type of setup? Sure, but it should only be used on show vehicles that don't see the road. Driving something like this is reckless and likely illegal in your area. Really, you're putting a loaded missile in the back of your vehicle, and no one wants that.

However, if you want a compromise, you have options. There are people who own hoppers that have essentially two setups. One is with standard-sized lines that run to a traditional tank and compressor setup. Then, there's another set that tees into the first, which is using the high-strength stuff. With the right plumbing and use of check valves, you could have two very interesting setups in one vehicle. It'd be expensive and not very practical, but you'd be able to hop your ride when you wanted.

Again, this isn't a recommended setup, but this book would be missing something if it wasn't mentioned. It is something you'll see out there in the wild, although it's far less common than it used to be.

Fittings

No matter which type of air setup you choose, you need fittings. They're the way to connect two components of different types. When running an air line from a valve to an airbag, you need fittings to make the transition from national pipe taper (NPT) on the fitting to push to connect (PTC) for the air line to possibly a compression fitting and NPT on the airbag. That's just one scenario.

Although this is a huge amount of fittings, it's also a good example of the kind of organization you want in your shop. After all, you're going to be using a lot of these little guys, and it'll help if you know where they are.

Fortunately (or unfortunately, depending on your perspective), there are many options. Some decisions will be based on aesthetics: chrome versus brass, plastic versus metal, etc. Others will be based on what you're connecting and how you want that connection made. You have many decisions to make, but there's a good place to start and that's with the materials used to make the fittings.

Materials

Every fitting has one or a combination of materials that make up the piece itself. Some are all metal. Others are metal and plastic, while another group is all plastic. What you select and where you put them makes a difference in the overall performance and longevity of the system.

Plastic fittings have their place. If you're running a line into the back of an air gauge, or you're placing the part in a low-heat environment, plastic fittings work well. Really, even in hotter spots (such as a trunk in the

This fitting has a brass base and plastic PTC fitting. Is it the right one for your build? Well, that depends.

summer) you'll be fine with a plastic fitting. However, if it's in the engine bay, steer clear. Similarly, if you live in a hotter environment like the Southwestern United States, plastic fittings won't last that long. Years? Sure. However, they break down like everything made from plastic in those parts of the country, and when they do, the system will leak.

From a longevity perspective, metal fittings are preferred. (Some fittings have metal bases but plastic inserts.) Brass, stainless steel, steel, and aluminum fittings are available, and they'll all work better than plastic if you want something that'll last a long time. However, not all metals are the same. Aluminum and brass are softer than steel and stainless steel. Sometimes, if a lower-quality metal fitting is used, the threads may not line up perfectly, which causes a leak. Also, if you're trying to connect two dissimilar metal fittings (for example: brass and stainless steel), you can easily strip out the softer one with the other or gall up the threads.

So, which type of fitting should you choose? It depends on the application and the location of the fitting. However, when in doubt, use one that's made by a reputable company (such as Parker, for example, which you can find at Grainger.com), and you'll be in good shape.

There's also one big thing on which to base all decisions moving forward: do you want D.O.T. or non-D.O.T. fittings?

D.O.T. versus Non-D.O.T. Fittings

The short answer to the question is easy: the U.S. Department of Transportation (or DOT, as you'll often find it listed online without the proper periods) has safety standards for any fitting that is used in an air brake system, such as those on a semi-truck. These are held to a higher standard than traditional fittings and air lines and have certain fail-safes in place to ensure that things don't go south for the wrong reason.

Of course, the longer answer is a bit more complicated.

When it comes to any line that connects to a fitting, the first sign that it's D.O.T. approved is on the

All D.O.T. fittings will have "D.O.T." stamped on the side. It's a federal requirement. If you buy fittings that say they're D.O.T. approved and they don't have this stamp, chances are good that they're fraudulent.

This is a disassembled D.O.T. PTC fitting. Notice that tube in the middle? It's what makes it a D.O.T. fitting.

side of the fitting itself. There is a "D.O.T." stamp in an obvious place. The second indication is inside. If you peer down into the area where the air line goes, there is a sleeve. That tube support would sit inside an air line, providing crush resistance if the line was bent or kinked. There are other regulations for tanks and lines as well, but to be concise, if you want your air system to have all the same components that you'd find in a semitruck's air brake system, use D.O.T. fittings.

This brings up the other question: do you really need D.O.T. fittings?

Not necessarily. If you're buying quality fittings and plan the air line routes carefully, then you could get away with not running D.O.T. fittings at all. In fact, there are some shops that sell the European equivalent of D.O.T., and they've never had issues. The argument could be made that D.O.T. fittings are nice but not a requirement for your air system.

Of course, you also risk thinking that you're buying quality fittings, but it turns out that they're garbage. Or, it could be that your air line isn't as nicely run as you thought, and there are a few kinks here and there. There could be any number of other reasons that could come up to change your situation.

So, in the end it's up to you. There's nothing wrong with running a non-D.O.T. approved fitting, and it could work just fine, and it's not like D.O.T. fittings can't fail because that can happen too. It's a matter of whether or not you want that extra assurance. There's no wrong answer here when it comes to fittings. It's your personal preference.

PTC Fittings

PTC fittings are a popular type for connecting air line to another item. However, to understand it, you need to see one that has been taken apart.

PTC fittings are very convenient to use, and as such, they are used in various air systems mostly because they're reusable. Let's say that you run an air line from the tank to a valve and you use a PTC fitting on both ends. Then, you change your

This is a PTC fitting seen from the side. The groove on the right-hand side is where the air line goes.

mind and decide that the route you chose for the lines is too treacherous, so you rerun it. Do you need to replace those fittings now? No. Just push in the end of the PTC fitting to release the collet and pull the air line out. It's easy.

The catch here is that different fittings have different qualities. Some fittings have plastic PTC ends and others have stainless steel or brass ends. Some valve manifolds even have plastic fittings pressed in place, and you can't change them. So, which is better, plastic or metal? Most of the time it comes down to personal opinion. However, plastic will break down faster over time (because of exposure to heat) than metals, so keep that in mind.

The other issue is leaking. Some PTC fittings leak because the collet isn't holding the line snug enough or the line isn't pressed tightly against the seal to keep things in place. Also, if there's any wiggle room between the line and the seal or if vibrations cause the line to move, that seal can leak too.

The bottom line is that PTC fittings offer flexibility and ease of use,

and they're widely available. You might be completely leak-free, or there could be issues. Just weigh the good with the bad before starting, and make the decision from there.

Compression Fittings

Have you ever replaced the 1/4- or multi-turn angle valve on a toilet or under a sink? The basic idea is that there is a piece of bare copper pipe or cross-linked polyethylene (PEX) tubing coming out of the wall. You need to put a valve there to feed either the faucet or the toilet, and that seal needs to be tight. The fix? A compression fitting. That's what we're working with here too.

These are the basic components of a compression fitting. There's the nut on the top, the sleeve in the middle, and the fitting itself with the insert on the bottom.

If the fitting is taken apart, you'll see that air line insertion point, and right underneath it is a piece called the collet. When you push the air line into the fitting, it moves past the collet and sits against a rubber O-ring. Once the line is pressurized, the collet keeps the line solidly connected and won't allow it to pull out.

Here's how everything looks from an exploded perspective when you put some 1/2-inch hose in the mix. The line goes through the nut and sleeve and then over the insert. Once it is tightened down, the sleeve compresses, locking the fitting tight.

Compression fittings are different than PTCs. There are three components: a nut, a sleeve, and the fitting itself. To assemble one, slide the air line through the nut, then the sleeve, then into the fitting. When the nut is tightened, the sleeve compresses, which seals the connection tight.

The advantage here is that you don't have to worry about your air line going anywhere. They're considered stronger than some PTC connections (depending on the quality of the PTC fitting), and they're easy to install.

However, that's where the convenience ends. The big problem with compression fittings is that they're one-time use only. Once that sleeve is crushed it's done, and it's not easy to remove, either. The only option is to cut the line off before the sleeve, and that may not leave you enough room to work with, depending on the way you arranged things. Think about that when you decide between compression and PTC fittings.

So, why would anyone use compression fittings over PTC for connecting air lines? The security of the lines is probably the main reason, and some just may not like worrying about PTCs. However, for lots of people, the one-time-use situation is a dealbreaker. It's also why many of the major valve manufacturers include PTC fittings on their own products.

It's often going to come down to a case-by-case basis. If you prefer the look and installation of compression fittings and you're not worried about having to replace them anytime soon, use them. As long as the air lines are solid and not leaking air, you'll be fine.

NPT Fittings

NPT describes how the threads themselves work. If you look at them up close, you'll notice that there's a taper to the threading itself that is different from the straight threads on the average bolt or nut. By having a taper, the threads eventually tighten against each other, making a theoretically tighter seal than with a straight thread pitch.

The problem is that it's not actually the case in systems that hold more than 60 psi. As a result, you use thread sealant on all NPT fittings, which is discussed more later

This is a D.O.T. fitting that's PTC on the right side and NPT on the left side. This fitting has orange thread sealant on the left, and some fittings come with it preinstalled.

Assembling Compression Fittings

The process of assembling compression fittings is pretty straightforward, but again, it's a one-time deal. That said, some people find it confusing, so here's a quick course in how it works. ■

The process begins by sliding the nut over the end of the cut air line and then the compression sleeve over that.

Then, the air line goes onto the fitting, and it's tightened in place.

Swagelok and Other Compression Fittings for Hard Lines

When you're putting together your airbag setup, something you'll debate is if you should run soft lines or hard lines. Further on in this chapter you'll receive more details on both, but if you decide to go with hard lines, you have to decide if you want to flare your fittings, install them with custom tools, or buy more expensive fittings.

In the case of the latter, you're looking at Swagelok fittings. There are a few similar options (for example, Gyrolok), but the idea is that you don't need to flare the tubing ends to install them into the fitting. Instead, they use special compression sleeves on the inside to tighten the seal.

These fittings are not cheap, but if you're going to hard line your setup, they make your life a lot easier. ■

These Hoke Gyrolok fittings work just like Swageloks, but they're a bit more affordable.

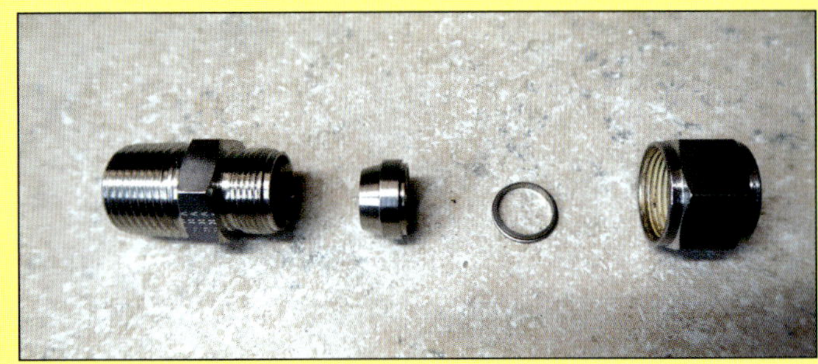

Inside each fitting are two compression sleeves. When used in the sequence shown, they can tighten down the line to the point that it'll be leak free.

in this chapter. For now, just know that either Teflon tape or Loctite 545/565 is your friend when using NPT fittings.

There are many different types of fittings out there, and they come in a lot of different shapes and sizes. You're going to use a lot of them in your build, and many will be NPT. Why? It's the best way to connect two fittings without the use of a separate line. You also might need one as a reducer to shrink the size of the necessary thread or to couple two air line fittings together.

Sealing Fittings

Thread sealant is an important part of the build process. It helps lock two connecting threads together,

This is an NPT reducer bushing, which, in this case, is 1/2 to 1/8 inch. You'd use this if you wanted to put one end in a cross and run an 1/8-inch PTC fitting for an air gauge or something similar.

This is an NPT female fitting, which means it has female NPT threads. It's called an elbow because of its 90-degree angle.

These are called cross fittings, and they are all female NPTs.

This is a weird-looking fitting. It's an NPT muffler, and it's designed to go into the end of a dump valve. This will slow down and quiet the air exiting the valve, which is nice if you want to either slow down your drops or tone down the noise.

This is a straight NPT threaded cylinder, and it's called a close nipple. If you see the same thing with a wrench end in the middle, that is a hex nipple.

If there is an extra hole in a tank that you need to plug, you'd use this fitting, which is the appropriately named NPT plug.

This is a branch T. If it was all the same end, it would just be a T-fitting, but the NPT base here makes it a branch T (If the NPT or dissimilar end was on one of the opposing ends of the T, it would be called a street T).

creating an air-tight bond in the process. It's always a one-time use thing because once you loosen the threads, that bond is gone. But hey, sealant isn't expensive, and it's good insurance against leaks.

Of course, there are many various threads that you'll encounter. NPT threads come to mind, as do those on compression fittings and even some AN fittings that might sneak their way into your life in other ways. Which ones do you seal?

It's pretty simple: You only seal NPT fittings. In a strange twist, sealing any other type of fitting with a thread sealant will actually *cause* it to leak, which is obviously the wrong thing to do. So, if you want a leak-free setup, use sealant only on NPT fittings.

So, what do you use to seal NPT threads? Either use Teflon tape/sealant or Loctite 545/565.

Teflon tape is a common household item if you do any kind of home repair, and it's used for plumbing in the same type of scenario you'd use for working under your sink. If you've done any kind of work around pipes in your house, you've probably used it before. It's a thin material that's just like tape in application, you just have to install it in a certain fashion.

Another option is liquid Teflon, which works the same way as Teflon tape but in a viscous application. Apply some onto the threads, and

NPT Fittings and Leaks

At this point, you know that NPT fittings have a tapered connection with the theory being that two NPT fittings tighten against each other to create a tight seal. That does happen, but you also need some kind of sealant to complete the bond, such as Loctite 545 or Teflon tape/paste. Without one of those, you're guaranteed to leak.

The thing is, you might be guaranteed to leak anyway, depending on what you're doing.

If you're putting together two different kinds of metals, one is probably stronger than the other. So, if you're turning a brass fitting into a steel tank, the brass is softer and could distort while you're tightening it in place. Also, you could have two fittings that are made of the same material, but because you tighten them so hard, they actually stretch the threads. This is something that happens with engine bolts all the time, and you have to consider it with your fittings too.

To complicate things further, all the connections between two objects that need to be solid-mounted together use NPT fittings: valve to valve, pressure switch and gauge lead to tank. Also, if every NPT fitting has the possibility to leak, then it stands to reason that the more NPT connections you have, the risk of having leaks is higher.

This doesn't have to derail your process, and you can use NPT fittings if you're installing them properly. However, know that if you don't (or even if you do), you can't just break them apart and reuse them because they may have stretched. Try to minimize the number of connections in your system, always make sure to use the proper sealant, and if you have a leak, check the NPT connections first. ■

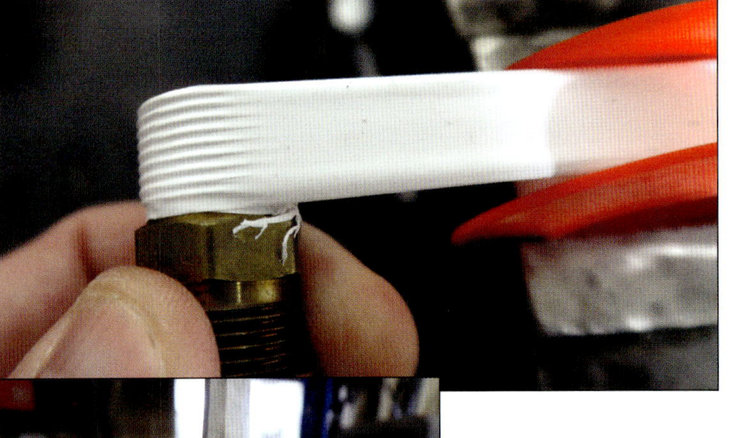

Teflon tape must be wrapped counterclockwise tightly around the threads. Otherwise, it will unspool as you tighten the fitting.

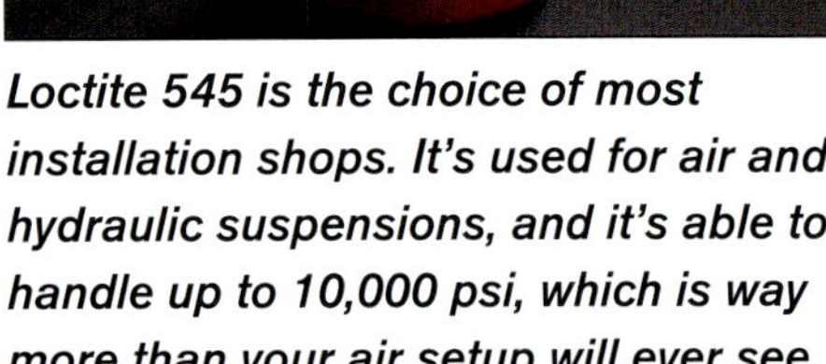

For what it's worth, most air suspension installation shops use and sell Loctite 545. It's a reddish-purple color and is so easy to use that it's silly not to. It's also faster to apply than Teflon tape and has less of a learning curve. Just put a few drops of it on the threads, and it'll work its way into the two connecting fittings as they are tightened together.

Properly Assembling NPT Fittings

On the surface, NPT fittings are pretty easy to install. After all, they're just male and female ends, and you just screw one into the other. But again, NPT fittings are also where you're most likely to get leaks, so you need to do things properly.

Before assembling, do a quick check of all your fittings. Make sure they're free of debris or burrs. Otherwise, you could strip the threads. Also, check the manufacturer of your fittings' website, as it may have specific recommendations on thread engagement and torque specifications.

it'll work its way into the fittings. Teflon tape is cleaner, as liquid Teflon never really dries totally. However, the choice is up to the user.

On the other side of the fence is Loctite 545 and 565. In both forms, it's a liquid sealant that's applied to the threads. Then, once dry, it seals everything up nice and tight. The main difference is the viscosity of the product, as 565 is thicker and comes in a smaller container.

Finally, there's traditional blue Loctite. It's not common, but some builders swear by the stuff and don't see any leaks. It may not be the recommended choice, but it could help out in a bind.

Loctite 545 is the choice of most installation shops. It's used for air and hydraulic suspensions, and it's able to handle up to 10,000 psi, which is way more than your air setup will ever see.

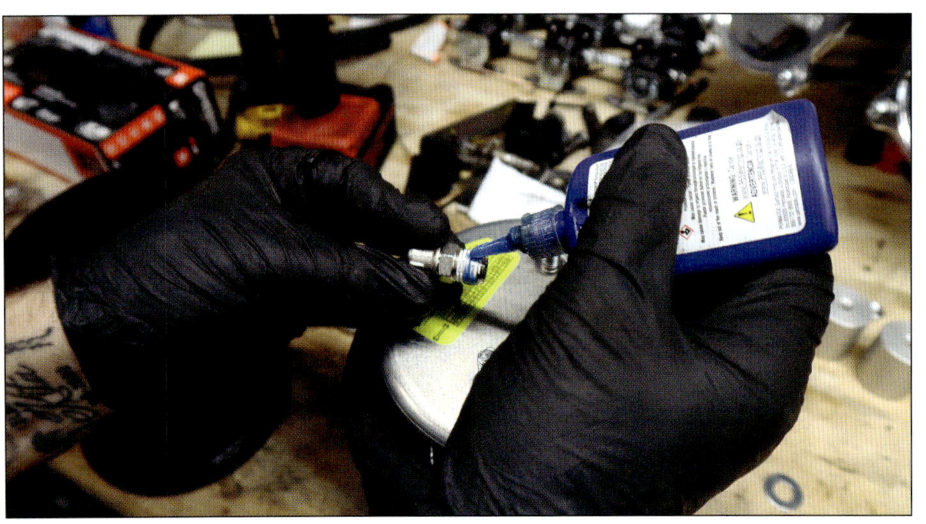

Yes, that's blue Loctite going on a fitting. Some of the crew at Switch Suspension swear by it and rarely see leaks as a result. Your results may vary, but these guys have been doing suspension for years, so it's worth listening to their tips.

With one fitting in a bench vise, begin installing the fitting. Make sure that it's covered in an appropriate sealant (in this case, Teflon tape) and leave the last two threads bare.

Get the fitting hand tight.

Now, use a wrench to tighten the fitting the rest of the way. The fitting manufacturer has guidelines on how many threads should be engaged, but the general rule is three to six turns.

Air Lines

So, you have the tank and fittings, but now it's time to connect everything together. What do you use? Air line. As with most things involved in an airbag setup, it seems like it should be a simple decision, but it's not. At least most of the time it's not.

Sizes and Uses

Air line is air line, right? Not really. There's a lot going on when it comes time to pick out air line. For one, a decision must be made to use hard lines, soft lines, or a combination of the two. If you get soft lines, you need to pick between D.O.T. and non-D.O.T. as well as the diameter of the hose.

Let's break these down one by one.

I'll get into the specific differences between each type shortly, but for now, know that air lines are available in a hard form that you need to shape with tools, or they are available in a soft form where it's completely flexible just like a garden hose. If you choose soft lines, then you have a D.O.T. decision to make.

As with fittings, the D.O.T. approves certain lines for use on the road. Semitrucks regularly use D.O.T.–approved soft line in their air-brake systems and never have problems. If you're putting a few tons of machinery on the road, you need it to stop, and if you're trusting some flexible tubing, it must be good stuff, right?

That's also your decision to make, except on a smaller scale. Fortunately, it's not that difficult a call: Go with D.O.T. The cost difference is negligible, and the extra reliability is worth it anyway. For example, Switch Suspension sells 1/2-inch D.O.T.-approved air line for $0.95/foot, and 3/8-inch for $0.85. That's cheap insurance for your air ride setup, so don't stress about the cost.

Then, there's the diameter of the line itself. As a general rule, the larger the diameter of the air line that you use, the faster you will lift and lower. This is dependent on the size of the fittings that are used as well. Otherwise, the smaller points in the system choke everything down to that speed. The point is that if you want speed, bigger lines are a part of that kind of system.

Let's just lay it out so that you have an idea of what you can do with each size.

- 1/8-inch: Mostly used for gauges. Run one from a branch or T-fitting to your gauge pod, and you'll get an accurate reading from the tank or corner.
- 3/16-inch: Sometimes for gauges and sometimes for airbag feed lines but mostly for the former.

This 1967–1972 Chevrolet C10 uses 3/16-inch hard line to feed the airbags. Is it too small? Well, according to the builder, it's great going up and maybe a tick slow going down. Otherwise, there are no worries at all. Also, he's using AN fittings on the lines.

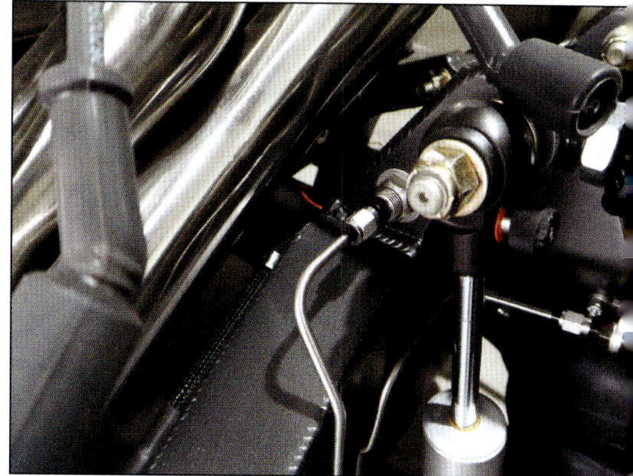

The 3/16-inch hard line also runs through the frame using a bulkhead fitting, which is a fitting that has a nut so that it can mount to something. This is very handy when you want to do a super clean install like this one.

- **1/4-inch:** This was popular in the early days, lost some steam in the 2000s, and now is picking back up. It's used to connect the valves to the airbags.
- **3/8-inch:** These are arguably the most common diameter air lines out there. Most D.O.T. 3/8- and 1/2-inch lines also have a nylon insert for extra strength and durability.
- **1/2-inch:** If you want speed, this is a good starting point. Systems with 1/2-inch lines pop up and down pretty quickly.
- **3/4-, 5/8- and 1-inch:** This size is for the dedicated hopper. It's difficult to fine tune your up and down movement with lines this big, but if you want to really take off, this is what you'll need.

Soft Line

Just like with hard line, the name here pretty much says it all. These types of air lines are flexible,

Here's some soft line spooled up and ready for use. The 1/2-inch line is up top, and 3/8-inch line is on the bottom.

although they are available in many different materials as well. The most common ones use a plastic composite, and you'll find rolls of those in custom car and truck shops across your town. Then, there are braided steel hoses, which are also technically soft lines and can be used with AN fittings. Finally, there are hydraulic hoses, which are a rubber-wrapped stainless-steel line designed for high pressures and are found in some airbag setups.

Why use soft line when hard line offers so many advantages? A soft line flexes, which means it can pop out of its mount, rub, and potentially rupture. It can burst just from pressure if you have a poorly rated line, and it's not as cool looking, either. So why use them at all?

Part of the answer is in the description: flexibility.

Imagine that you have a gauge pod in your driver-side pillar, and you need to run lines up to them. Do you really want to make a hard line? That would be a nightmare to bend, nevermind install. What if you're putting together your setup and just need to get the vehicle up and moving around the garage? Soft line is a ton faster to install, that's for sure.

However, the literal flexibility isn't its only advantage. There's also the price. Soft line is cheaper by far compared to hard line, plus it's easier to find locally. Ease of installation is another key factor. As previously mentioned, it's simpler to install in most scenarios than traditional hard line.

For most people, the decision is about cost. It is substantially cheaper than comparable aluminum or stainless-steel hard line (particularly once you add in the cost of tools), and it's much easier to install, so if

you're paying to have that done, you're going to save a ton of cash. As a result, soft line became the standard for most installers and consumers.

Mounting Soft Line

Since soft line is so easy to run and move, you would think it would also be equally easy to mount. For the most part, that's correct. However, there are still good and bad ways to do it.

The most popular way, anecdotally, is to use zip ties. They're quick, easy, and cheap, so many people use them. Zip ties have their place in the install process, but don't use them to hold up your lines for anything more than temporary measures—unless you use quality zip ties.

Traditional zip ties break. They dry rot, snap, and get brittle, which are all the things that you don't want them to do when they're holding something important in place. That also happens because soft lines can flex and shift when pressure runs through them. This constant movement can cause rubbing, and when a plastic soft line starts chafing against a hard plastic zip tie, it usually results in a puncture.

So, keep a set of zip ties in your toolbox, but don't rely on them every day—unless you splurge on the good ones.

What you can use are rubber-coated clamps. These are easy enough to find at your local hardware store, and they're not very expensive, either. All you do is wrap the clamp around your line, then bolt it in place. You'll have to drill a hole to mount them, but that's not a huge deal. Plastic clamps also work well, particularly with smaller lines.

Note that self-tapping screws are probably not the best idea. Although

These weather-resistant, high-performance cable ties by Ty-Rap are great. If you look close, you can see a metal tang. It ensures that the cable tie cinches tightly without breaking.

they function well, since those lines flex, the connection to the vehicle can loosen over time. Then, you'll end up with a line that's hanging down under your car or truck with a few hose clamps clustered at the base. Consider tapping the frame or body if possible, or use a Nutsert. Bolting your clamps to the chassis helps tremendously.

Another thing you can work with are line clips. These are similar to the Christmas-tree clips that hold a door

To take it to the next level, get yourself one of these. It's a Ty-Rap ERG50 cable tie tool. It's not cheap ($225 at Amazon), but it's made to dial in the clamping pressure for cable ties. It also ensures that you don't overtighten them, which is critical with air lines.

How to Properly Cut Soft Air Lines

Although it seems pretty obvious, there is a right and a wrong way to cut soft air lines, particularly if PTC fittings are used. That's because a straight and clean cut makes for a better seal and provides more surface area for the fitting to grab. If it's at too sharp an angle, half or more of the tangs on the inside of the fitting won't seat, and you'll have a leaky connection.

There are many different cutters out there, but sometimes the cheapest option is the best. Small air line cutters are affordable, easy to use, and serviceable if the blade needs to be replaced. The idea is to put the air line into the V-shaped groove on the bottom of the cutter and hold it as straight as possible. Then, push down on the top of the cutter, slicing the line.

If you're planning to do an installation with soft line, pick up a few of these and keep them around the shop. Use a chain or string to hold a spare one nearby your roll of line and have others just floating around your workspace. It never hurts to have one nearby.

More handheld options are available, and they work well too. However, if you're just starting out, having a tool like this one will make your life go a little bit smoother, and that's not a bad thing. ■

Cutters like these are the best and cheapest way to go. They are available for less than $10 from Switch Suspension, Parker, or AVS.

To cut the line, place it in the notch on the cutter, keep it straight, and clamp down, severing the tubing.

These Quick Clips hold both soft and hard line tubing (or any other kind of lines). They range in price from less than $1 to $1.76. (Photo Courtesy Switch Suspension)

panel to the sheet metal, except here they're designed to hold both soft and hard lines. They come in a variety of sizes, and all you have to do is drill a hole and push them inside.

Also, don't forget that soft line doesn't handle heat well. If you're running lines by your engine, make sure they're far enough away from a heat source that they don't warm up and rupture. Build a heat shield if necessary to make sure they stay cool.

Lines should not sit under the car or truck, either. So, if your vehicle sits on the ground, the air line shouldn't be between the concrete and your ride. Although that seems like it should be fairly obvious, it's quite often not, and you'd be surprised what you see in the wild.

Regardless of which method or combination of methods you use to get the job done, make sure that those lines stay secure. Check on them regularly, and if something seems loose, tighten it up. It's always better to be safe than sorry.

This is a tubing straightener, and it's important to have if you're working with coiled aluminum hard line. Otherwise, you risk mis-shaping the tubing.

There are marks on the bender that you use to line up each bend. There's also some spring-back to the metal depending on what you're using, so consider that when you're making your bends.

Hard Line

The argument could be made that using hard line for your air suspension is a great upgrade. Not only does it look good but it's also incredibly durable. The downside is that there is a steep learning curve.

Step back for a minute and look at the big picture. At this point, you know that you need some kind of connection running between the airbags and the valves. You've also learned that soft lines are flexible and easy to run. So, why would you run hard lines?

The first, and most obvious answer is insurance. If you're airbagging your vehicle, chances are good that you want it to be low. How low? Well possibly on-the-asphalt low, which means that your air lines will sit very close to the ground. If you have a bagged car or truck, you probably drive pretty low too. What happens if you lose a hose clamp on one of your soft air lines and it starts sag-ging down?

That's the first reason why people decide to install hard lines on an airbagged vehicle. It ensures that you won't drag through, pinch, or otherwise damage a soft line, which gives you one less thing to worry about. That's not to say that hard lines are impervious to all damage, but they're certainly more resilient than plastic.

The second reason is looks. They just look good when they're installed properly—to the point that there are

HOW TO INSTALL AIR RIDE SUSPENSION SYSTEMS

entire businesses dedicated to doing hard-line plumbing. You can turn a functional part of your suspension into art if you take your time, which many people do. All it takes is some creativity.

However, if it were easy, everyone would be doing it. To properly install hard line on your vehicle, you need several tools, including a hard line bender, a tubing cutter, and a deburring tool too. Once you have the tools, you need to properly bend the tubing, which involves learning how to use the bender. Since each tube has its own series of bends, it gets complicated fast. One wrong turn and you have to bend a whole new tube. Oh, and you'll need the right fittings too.

So, should you tackle hard lining your vehicle? Absolutely. It's not easy, and it won't be cheap. But the results are stellar.

Going into the hard line process, you need to know what kind of fittings you're going to use. You have a few options.

The first is AN. If you've ever done any fuel line plumbing on your truck, you've probably used AN lines. They have ends with a 37-degree flare, and you can make them yourself if you have the right tool. Then, you need the appropriate fittings for the flare (a nut and a sleeve). The sleeve goes next to the flare, and the nut goes over both the sleeve and the flare to make its connection.

Note that AN fittings do not require (nor should they have) any kind of thread sealant on them.

The second option is using specialized fittings. As mentioned earlier in this chapter, brands such as Swagelok and Gyrolok make compression fittings designed for hard line that don't require any special flaring.

All of the fittings on this chassis are Swagelok. However, pay attention to the area on the two tanks just to the left of center. Those will be used as a starting point for a hard-lining project in this chapter.

In fact, you don't technically need special tools, although you should probably consider buying some if you're doing it frequently.

A Swagelok fitting has multiple parts: the base fitting, two compression sleeves, and the nut at the end. Tightening Swagelok fittings isn't a difficult process, but the amount you turn the fitting depends on the diameter of tube. Swagelok has an excellent video on YouTube if you want to see it in action.

The basic idea is that you need to set one half of the fitting into a vise or an immovable object, such as a second wrench or something similar. Then, mark the nut with a permanent marker. Now, with a wrench, turn it the specified amount. Once that's done, check it with a tool you might want to buy, which is a Swagelok gap-inspection gauge. If the gauge fits, tighten the fitting down further.

Unlike traditional compression fittings, you can reuse Swagelok fittings, which is very good news if you need to sort something out down the line. The downside? They're not cheap. Scientific Instrument Services (Sisweb.com) sells a 1/4 to 1/4 MPT (male NPT) fitting in stainless steel for $12.95 each. Picking up eight of those will set you back just over $100, so it's not inexpensive. However, it does make the hard line installation process a lot easier, so you may want to weigh your time against the cost.

The final option involves PTC fittings, but it's a bit more complicated than just pushing the line into the fitting as you'd traditionally do.

Most of the time, you want to do the hard line in stainless steel. It's prettier, you can polish it up nice, and it's super strong. However, stainless steel is a hard metal, and the way a PTC fitting is designed, it needs to grip its tangs into the air line to be able to lock it in place. If the fitting is made of a metal that's softer than stainless steel (which most are), you'll never get the two to work together.

f you've ever bent and flared your own brake lines, making an AN flare is going to be a piece of cake. If that's not the case, it may seem intimidating. However, it's not bad if you have the right tools. ■

This is an Earl's Performance 001ERL vise-mount flaring tool, and it costs about $420 on Amazon or $469 at Jegs and Summit. It makes flaring and double flaring hard lines easy.

1 *Mount the flaring tool into a bench vise. Those two darker gray pieces in the middle clamp the tube.*

2 *This is a turret-style flare tool, so it has multiple ends. In this case, it's a 37-degree single flare for AN fittings.*

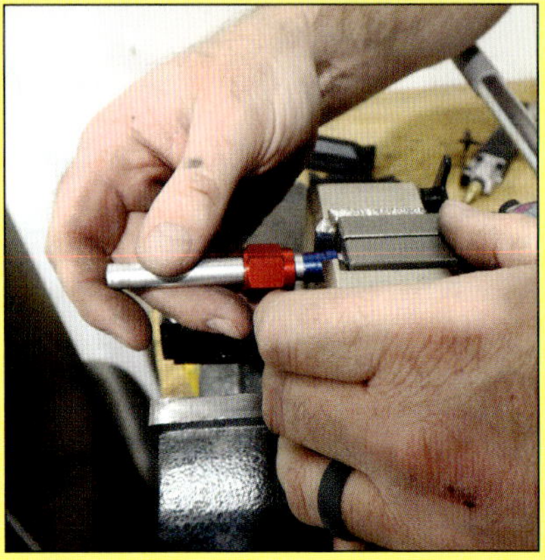

3 *The tubing is now put into the center section and clamped into place. The blue part on the tubing is the sleeve, and the red is the nut. If this line was already bent, it would be critical to have the sleeve in place. Otherwise, it won't fit around a bend, and you'll have to start over.*

4 *With the tubing flush to the gate, the first operation of the flare tool is performed. It pushes the tubing back to the proper place to be flared correctly. Once it's done, the line can be tightened down all the way.*

5 *A little grease helps lubricate the tip, which makes it easier for the flaring process to happen smoothly.*

6 *The flare is set by first tightening the line in the vise and then clamping down on the lubricated flare tip.*

7 *The completed flare with nut and sleeve is now ready to be installed onto an AN fitting.*

How do you make that connection?

Here again, you have a choice. You can use aluminum instead of stainless steel, but it has its drawbacks. For one, you need to find some aluminum line that's pretty soft, yet still strong enough to hold the pressure. It usually comes in rolls, so you want a special tool to straighten it out called a tubing straightener (Eastwood sells them for $89 each, and they're size specific). You can bend and distort the tubing when you cut it, making the whole process go south on you pretty quick. However, that shouldn't discourage you from using aluminum hard line, you just need to be aware of the drawbacks.

There is a way to make a PTC connection work with stainless, and it's one of those trade secrets that many people don't want to talk about. However, once you know it, it'll save you a ton of time.

Modifying Stainless-Steel Tubing to Work with a PTC Fitting

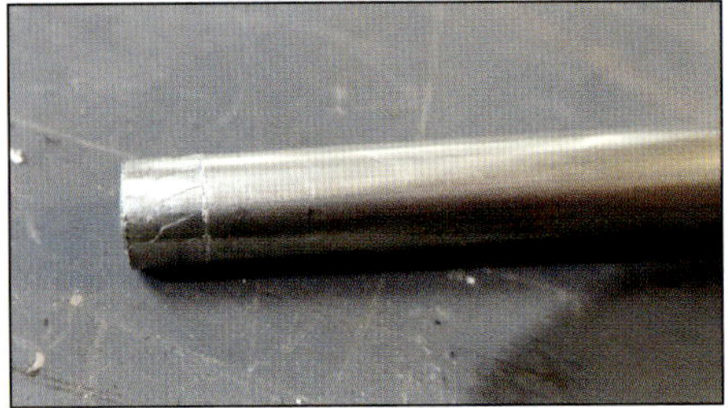

1 *Everything begins with a test. Take some soft aluminum tubing of the same diameter as the stainless steel and push it into the desired PTC fitting. Pull it back hard until it bites. Then, depress the end of the PTC to release the aluminum line and inspect the end. This is the mark you'll see.*

2 *Now, take a pair of calipers and use them to measure the distance between the end, or face, of the tube and those marks. Then, lock the calipers down so they can't move.*

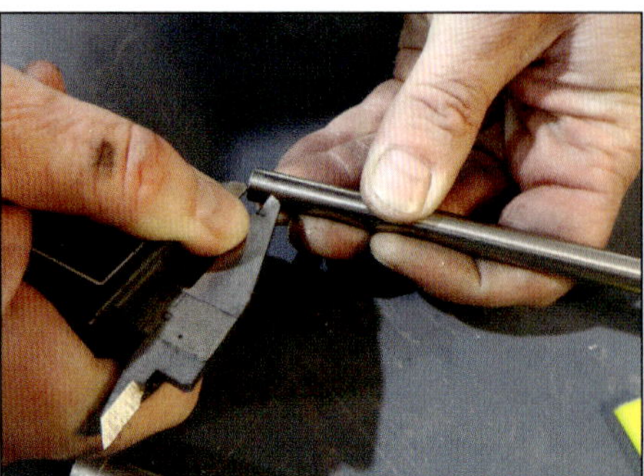

3 *Use the calipers to scribe the end of the stainless-steel tubing at the same point where the PTC gripped on the aluminum. You can also use a permanent marker to make the marks more visible, if necessary.*

4 *This is where the secret sauce is made. Now, you need to create a bead roll in the tubing at the PTC mark. To do that, modify a traditional tubing cutter to look like this.*

5 *What you're doing is flattening the cutter blade and then just slightly chamfering the edges so that it won't cut. To do that, just remove the clip, pull out the blade and grind it down on a sander or something similar.*

6 *Work the modified cutter around the marked spot on the tubing just like you would if you were cutting it, but keep an eye on the depth. Once you have enough that you think will work, pull the line out of the modified cutter.*

7 *The tubing is now all set for a traditional PTC fitting. Do this depth test exercise with every new fitting you use because it won't always be the same.*

Bending Hard Line Tubing

No matter which way you go, you're going to have to bend your hard line at some point. This is something that makes a lot of people nervous because hard line is expensive, making mistakes pricey. After talking to people who do this for a living, one tip became clear: if you screw up, use that piece for reference.

Cut off the mistake bend and save it for later. It provides a framework for how a tube should go and an idea of whether or not a particular bend will fit in a specific spot. It's all reference. That, and you will have waste in this process no matter what, so get used to that.

Another tip? Your bender has a direction of sorts. That means if you want to duplicate a bend, you should bend things holding the bender in the same orientation as the previous one, feeding the line in using the same positioning. It also helps to think three dimensionally when orienting the bends and to visualize where the tubing will land once it's molded to its final position.

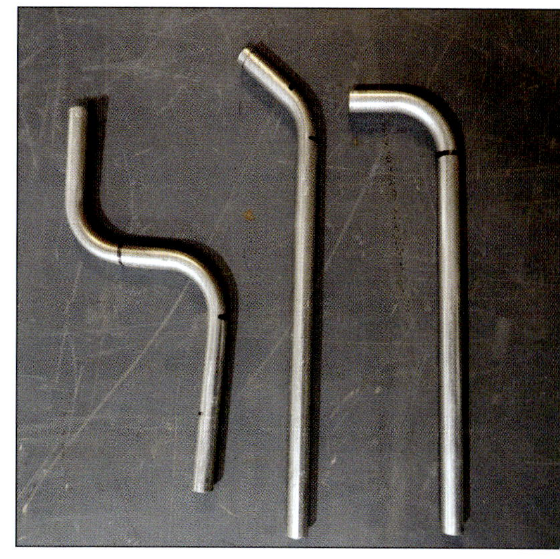

Keep scrap bent pieces (such as these) for reference, and when you need to test fit a bend, use them instead.

Preparation for Bending

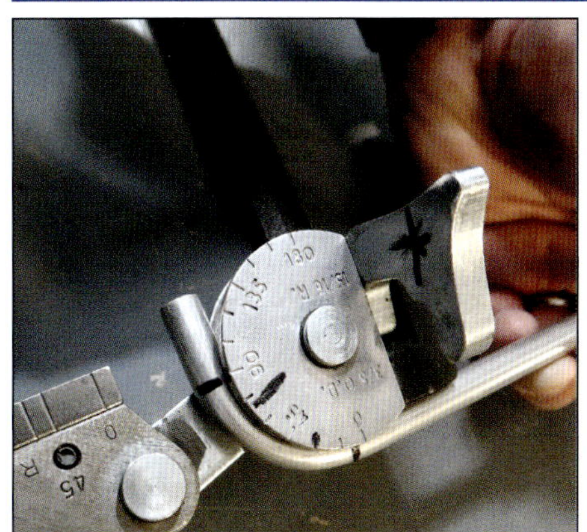

1 Before you start bending, always note your starting point and angles on your lines with a permanent marker. Then, you'll know the angle later when you're duplicating them on other sides.

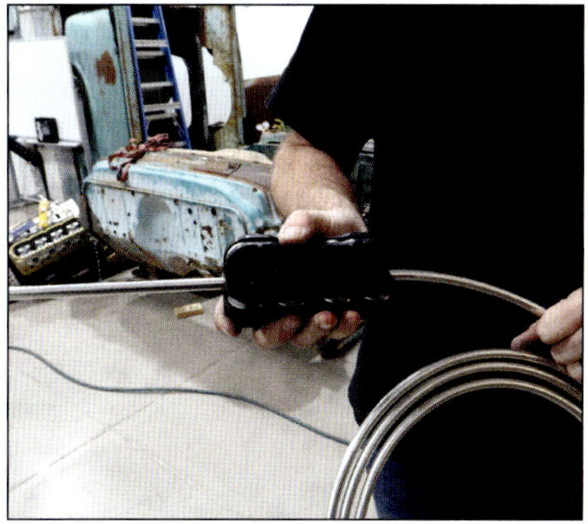

2 The process begins with straightening out the aluminum tubing. This handheld pipe-straightening tool is made by Kwix UK, and you can get it on Amazon for about $90 in various sizes.

3 A rough estimate is made to see how much tubing is needed, and then it's cut off with a tubing cutter. To do that, put the tubing in the grips and tighten the cutter down a little bit. Run the cutter around the tubing, tighten slightly, and repeat until it severs.

4 The problem is that the cutter will deform the tubing slightly inward, creating a burr. To get rid of the burr, clean it out.

5 A quick pass with a chamfer bit will clean out that burr and provide a nice starting point for a flare if you decide to go that direction.

Starting to Bend

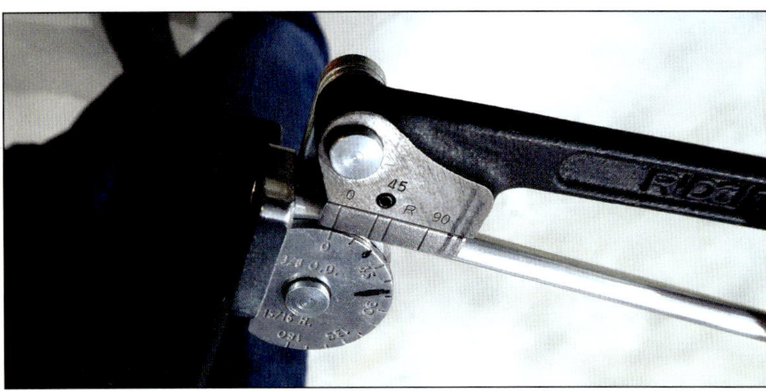

1 To begin correctly, do these two things: 1) line up the "0" on the dial on the bender with the "0" on the die part of the bender, and 2) make sure that the end of the tube is at a consistent spot. In this case, Jason from Arizona High Test knows that putting it at the end of the tube holder is good enough for his Swagelok fitting, so that's his starting point.

2 Now, he bends the tubing by pulling the die arm across the bender until the hash by the "0" on the die lines up with the angle he wants. In this case, it's 90 degrees.

3 Here's the other critical part: he now marks the beginning and end point of those bends with a permanent marker. This ensures that later, when he needs references, he has them.

Test Fitting the Tubing

1 With the tubing pushed in place, he now marks the bottom of the tubing with a permanent marker. This is his reference point for where he wants the bottom of the tubing to sit, and he'll mate that with the bottom of the bender.

2 Here's how that mark lines up with the bender. You don't have to do it this way, but having a mark on the top or bottom of the tube is a very nice reference to have.

Test Fitting the Tubing *continued*

3 The bending process is repeated now for the 45-degree bend, aligning the "0" with the 45-degree mark. Then, everything is marked again with a permanent marker.

4 You can probably tell where this goes from here. But how does he know where to bend the tube to match what was done previously?

Matching the Bends

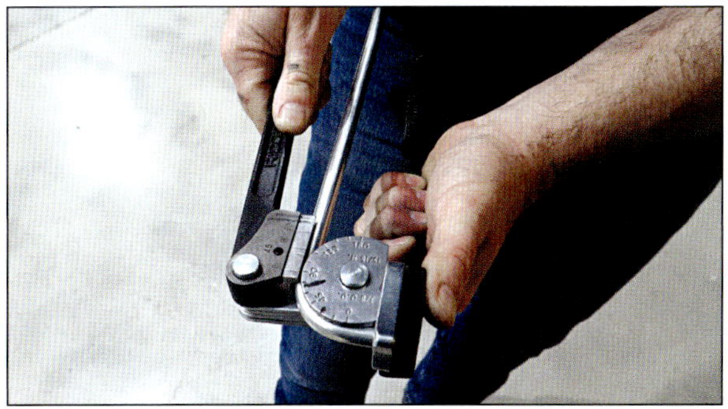

1 The easiest way is to duplicate the line that was already made is with another piece of scrap. That's what he does next.

2 Now those reference marks come in handy. Using those as a guide, he roughly measures the distance between where he bent the 90 and the 45.

3 Those measurements are then transferred over to the new scrap piece of tubing, and then the bends are matched. Now, he has two matching pieces of bent line.

4 With both bends in place, the marks made on the scrap piece are transferred over to the good piece with a permanent marker. Now he knows where to bend the 45 and what direction it needs to go.

Making Final Bends

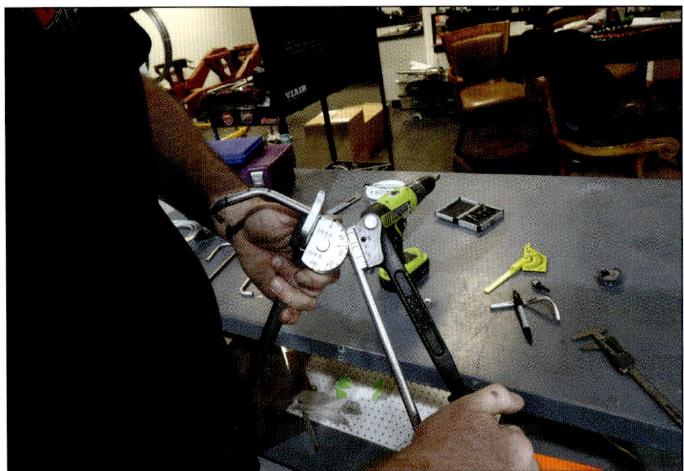

1 *The 45-degree bend is now bent in place and again marked with a permanent marker just in case.*

2 *The final bend mark is transferred from the first using the calipers and a permanent marker.*

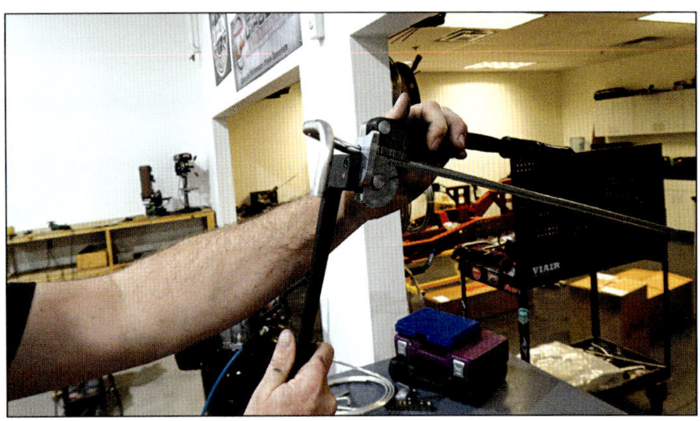

3 *Lining things up can be tricky, but again, just hold it out and visualize where the bend will go. If you take the time to do that, you will be fine.*

4 *The final 90-degree bend is then put in place.*

Completing the Installation

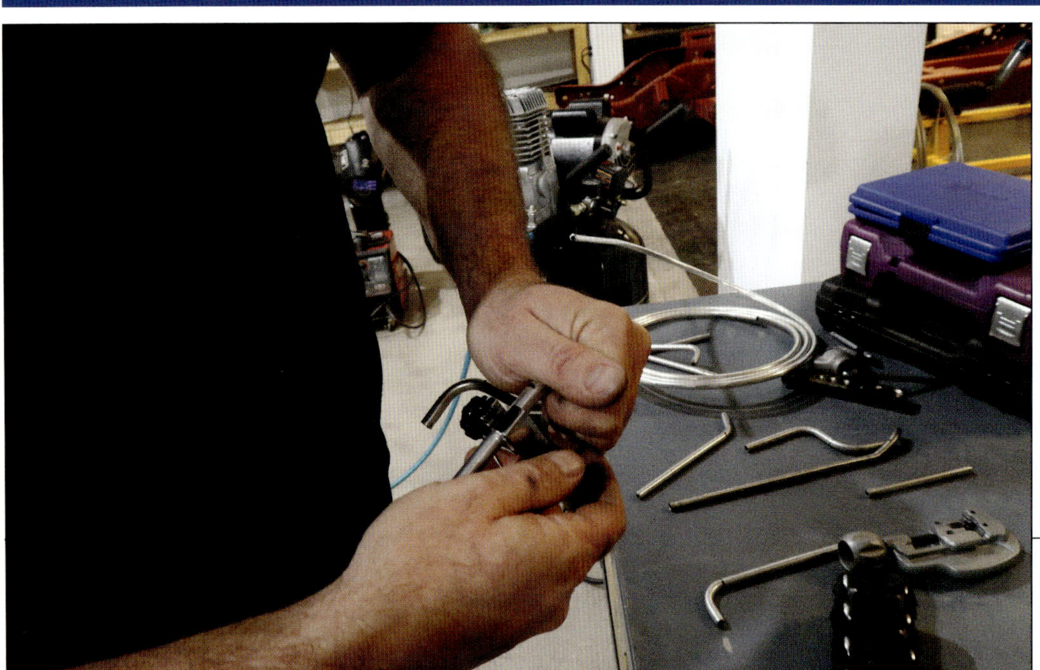

1 *The last step is to cut the tube down to size, and to chamfer the end to deburr it.*

Completing the Installation *continued*

2 *Everything is now pushed into the Swagelok fittings to ensure proper fitment.*

3 *It fits perfectly. Now, the fittings just have to be cinched down, and it will be airtight.*

4 *Before that happens, how do you remove the permanent marker? Just spray a little bit of brake cleaner on the marks, and they'll wipe right off.*

Mounting Hard Line Tubing

You might ask yourself why you would want to mount your hard line tubing at all. It is rigid, and once it's set in place, it's not going to move, right? Before the question is answered, go ahead and look beneath your vehicle and locate the gas and brake lines. Are those hard lines mounted? Right. So should your hard lines.

As with many things, there are many ways to do this. Doing a hard line installation means that you want a cleaner look anyway, so you should probably make sure how your lines are secured is clean as well. Zip ties work but should only be used for quick fixes.

Instead, use hose clamps and specialty clips. There's a company named NotcHead that sells hard line clamps that are easy to install and look amazing. A six pack of 3/8-inch clamps sells for $21. The company makes them for soft lines too, which makes the installation process go a lot smoother.

You can also use rubber hose clamps just like you would with soft lines. However, since hard lines are designed to be very organized and pretty, weigh your options. Make sure that whatever method you choose, it's right for your build.

VALVES

So far, this book has provided an overview of how airbag systems work: what compressors are and how they function; tanks, fittings, and air lines; and now, it's on to the valves. In a nutshell, valves are the way that air gets from the tank to the airbags and then back out into the atmosphere. Without them, an airbag setup isn't truly functional.

However, there isn't just one type of valve. There are many different styles available, and you could use one or more of them in a single installation. To understand how and why, let's break down some of the basics.

Valve Types

The simplest and most basic type of valve that you'll find on an airbag installation is called a Schrader valve. If you've ever put air in your tires, you know what one of these looks like, and in the airbag world, it serves the same purpose: to allow an outside device to put air into an object and then provide a way to let air out.

At its most complex, there are valve manifolds. These are machined blocks of aluminum that hold multiple valve bodies in one chunk.

They allow you to save space and fittings by consolidating everything together, and they're usually pretty straightforward to plumb and wire. However, they're more expensive.

A valve, no matter the price, is there just to allow you to get air in and out of an object. Some of them are manual and some are electric. Both do the same thing, and they both have their place.

Let's break it down even further, though.

Manual

Going back to the tire example, a Schrader valve is the most simple version of the manual valve. There are no electrical requirements to get them going. It's all about what you manually put in and take out.

You might think that a Schrader valve has no place in your install, but that's not correct. For one, they're quite popular when you're mocking everything up. Just put a T-fitting between two soft lines connected to the airbags and install a Schrader valve in the middle. Then, use shop air to lift up your project, even if nothing electrical is mounted. You can even buy a Schrader valve with a PTC fitting.

This is a Schrader valve. In this case, it has a PTC fitting at the other end to connect it to the air line.

Another option for a Schrader valve is to mount one directly onto your tank. Let's say the relay to your compressor goes south, and you need to put air in your system. Shop air to the rescue (or gas station air if you're away from your own workshop). It may sound like a weird idea, but it's been done for sure.

The next step up in manual valve complexity is either a manual toggle air valve or a manual paddle air valve. Both of these do the same

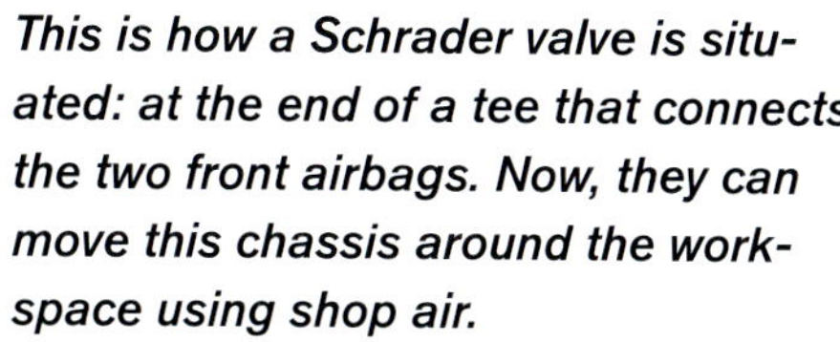

This is how a Schrader valve is situated: at the end of a tee that connects the two front airbags. Now, they can move this chassis around the workspace using shop air.

The back of the manual paddle switch has two spots for air. With these, one leads to the tank, and one goes to the bag for lifting purposes. If you want to let the air out, you'll need a second paddle switch. Then, one of the ports is empty, and the other line goes to the bag. That usually means you'll require a T-fitting to connect the bag line to the two paddle switches.

This is a manual toggle air valve. It has spots for fittings on the bottom and sides so that you can plumb it correctly into the system.

This is a manual paddle switch. It serves the same purpose as the toggle, but it's a paddle-style switch instead.

thing: a hose running from the tank is inserted into one end and another line running to the bag on the other. By either toggling the switch or holding the paddle, you're manually allowing air to go into the airbag.

These are both great options for new installations for a few reasons. First, they're cheap. Manual paddle valves are $25 at Switch Suspension, and even though you'd want eight (four for up, four for down), it eliminates the sometimes-complex issue of wiring your valves, and that's a time saver. Also, they're good for test-ing out your setup. Build yourself a quick panel with some MDF or scrap steel and use it during the mock-up phase. You could even keep it around the shop for future installs.

As a whole, manual valves should be viewed as a waypoint on your air suspension journey. You don't have to stop there if you don't want, but if you do, it could help.

Electric

Ultimately, this is most likely what you'll use for your valves. Although electric valves need to be

This is an SMC valve, and it's a great example of a reliable, high-quality valve.

Looking closer at the body, you can see that there's a direction of flow marked on it. This is the way you want that valve to run, so make sure you plumb it accordingly.

wired up, they're a great solution to the problem of how to get air to your airbags. They come in two basic forms.

The first is an individual valve. Although these were common in the past, they're not as popular as they used to be for reasons that will come up later. Basically, the idea is that you'll need two valves per corner: one to lift and one to lower. Each valve is directional, and if you want, you can also plumb in a line for a gauge.

The advantage with running a setup like this is that if you have a valve fail, you can just replace the individual valve and not the entire assembly. That's one factor, and an individual valve is cheaper than the alternative, which is a valve manifold.

On the downside, these things turn into mammoth pieces of kit with lots of expensive fittings being spent up in the process. They're also harder to find today as previously mentioned, so take that into consideration. Although individual valves are cheaper than manifolds, you need to buy eight valves for one setup plus the fittings, and that is more expensive

Here's the initial valve setup. These particular models have a top and bottom for different speed ratings. The one on the left is for the exhaust, and the on for the right is for lift.

Each fitting is assembled as follows: a few drops of Loctite 545 is put on the threads, one fitting is put into a bench vise, and then the other is tightened in place until firm. The process is repeated until the entire assembly is complete.

The little fitting that's been put into the side of this branch tee is for plumbing the gauge with 1/8-inch air line.

This is an example of a completed assembly. It's big, but all the valves are easily accessible yet hidden from view.

cumulatively. In addition, all of those fittings are NPTs, which introduce more opportunities for leaks.

Wiring a Valve

There are many different types of electric air valves out there, but they usually come with two or three connectors at the end. As if that wasn't easy enough to deal with, the connectors typically aren't specific to any one power source, which means that you can wire 12-volt positive to either the left or right terminal. It just doesn't matter.

Let's back up for a moment and explain some of the basics of automotive electrical systems. A car or truck is wired with direct current (DC) power. This means that you have a positive and a negative (also called a ground), and both need to be connected to function. The positive connection usually traces back to the vehicle's positive terminal on the battery via a fuse block or something similar, and the negative connection can go to any bare-metal surface on the car.

These Asco valves have three prongs up top. The top two are interchangeable between 12-volt positive and ground, but the bottom isn't used in air suspension applications. (Photo Courtesy Switch Suspension)

So that's it, right? Well sure, but no. There's another thing to consider, which might be familiar to you if you've ever wired up a car stereo: ignition power.

The typical automotive electrical system has constant power (something that's tapped directly into the battery) and switched power (which only turns on with the ignition). Your car stereo, for example, is wired to both constant and ignition. It's able to remember your radio presets and the time via constant power, but the ignition lead actually turns it on.

Why is all this important? Well, if everything in your car ran on constant power, it would kill the battery shortly after the engine was turned off. If it was all on ignition, anything with any kind of memory would be wiped out daily like they're the actor Guy Pearce in the movie *Memento*.

With wiring the compressors, you usually want to connect the relays to ignition connections. That way, the compressors don't kick on when the car or truck is turned off, draining the battery in the process. The switches, on the other hand, can go either way. The safer option is still to keep it on ignition power so that you don't risk leaving a switch triggered overnight and cause a fire. However, it's ultimately your call.

Finding the ignition lead is another thing altogether. There are a few obvious places to look: the ignition itself and the back of your vehicle's stereo. Both are fused connections, and since you're not pulling much power from them, you should be fine.

You can also use a multimeter to find an open connection in your fuse block. Oftentimes, the car you buy doesn't have every option under the sun, and there are blank spots where

you can tap in. Just make sure to test and make sure it's not constant power.

Finally, if you want the benefits of both constant and ignition power, you can always connect your valves via a switch panel to a dedicated power switch. This toggle switch is an on-off style where you can connect constant power to the center and then the valves to the other end. In this way, you can turn on the valves even if the vehicle isn't running and just keep them off otherwise. In fact, some people do this and use a red aircraft safety cover like you'd find in the cockpit of an F-16. Whenever the cover is down, the switch is off, and therefore you're safe. Just flick open the cover and trigger the switch to turn it on.

How to Make Connections

As you run the wiring to your valves, you'll find that at one point or another you need to make a connection. Sometimes it's a bundle of wires that can be joined via a fancy waterproof harness, but more likely, it's just two wires that need to be spliced. You have a few options to do so.

If you're creating a junction point for your wiring, one option is a terminal block.

In a typical wiring job, many people run a bundle of wires from

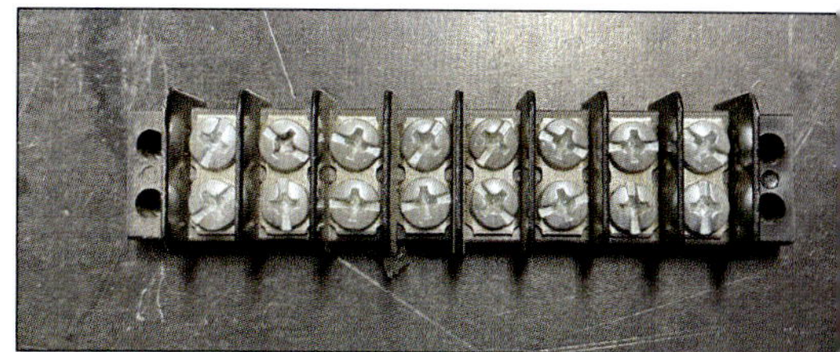

Terminal blocks such as this are handy if you want to create a junction point for all of the wiring for easy disassembly.

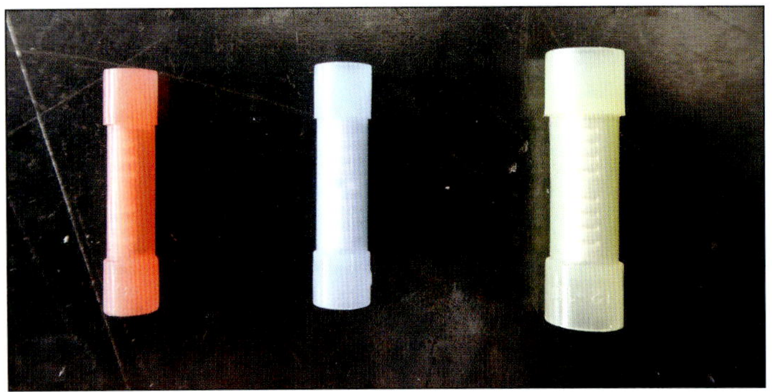

Butt connectors are great for quick connections. If you get the kind with heat-shrink ends, they can be waterproof as well.

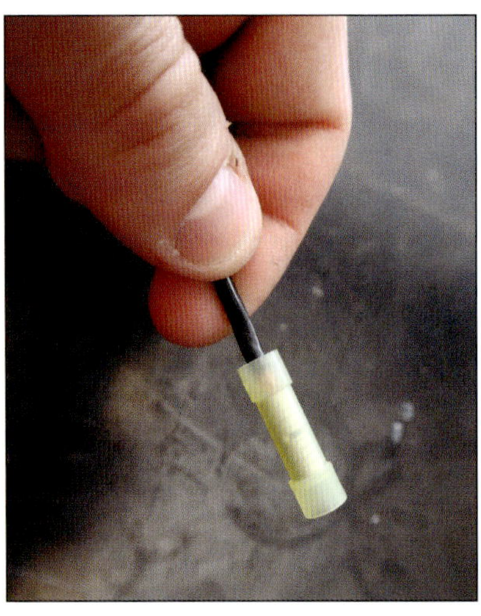

To start a crimped connection, strip about 1/4 inch off the end of the wire with a wire stripper. Then, insert the bare wire into the center of the butt connector.

Hold the butt connector in the jaws of a crimping tool so that it's over the side with the wire that needs to be crimped, but also in the middle. That's where the metal that actually joins the two wires together sits, and if you just crimp the plastic part, it won't hold.

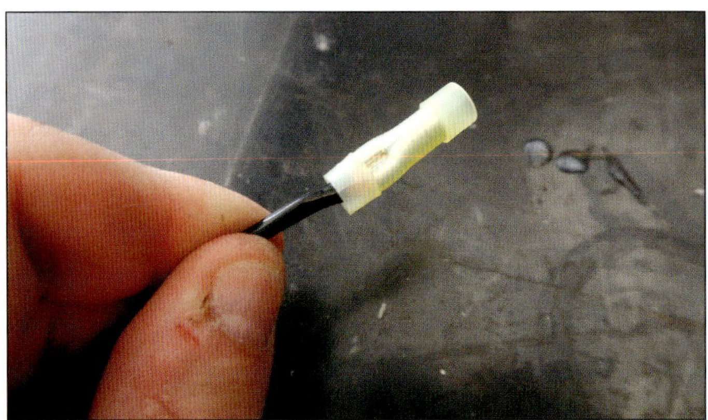

A completed crimp looks like this. You should be able to hold the butt connector in one hand and the wire in the other, and tug. If the wire doesn't move, there is a solid connection.

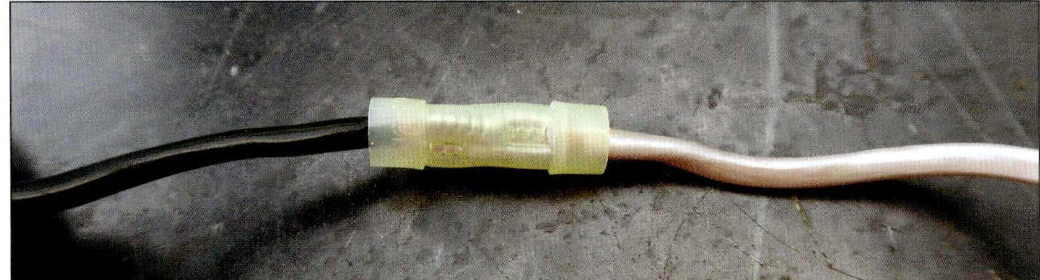

With both ends crimped, the connection is complete. At this point, assuming that you planned ahead, you can cover the joint with heat shrink tubing to seal it tight. Otherwise, you can call the connection done and move on to the next one.

the switch box back to the valves and then splice, solder, or butt connect them directly in place. What if you ever need to service that valve or maybe just take off the body and get some work done? If the valve doesn't have spade connectors or some kind of harness, you're in for a world of hurt.

A terminal block provides a spot for all of your connections to feed into. Your wiring can be terminated with spade connectors or just bare wire and screwed right in. Then, should you need to service anything in your setup, you can just unscrew one of the points on the block and remove the wire.

Another option is using butt connectors. These come in three colors: red, blue, and yellow. Red connectors are for 18- to 22-gauge wire, blue are for 14- to 16-gauge wire, and yellow are for 10- to 12-gauge wire. In an air suspension setup, you'll typically use blue for the valves and yellow for the compressors. This color-coding pattern also applies to crimped spade connectors and the like.

Some people speak ill of the butt connector, and there are a number of reasons why. If you don't get a solid crimp, you won't have a good connection, and that means you'll have electrical problems. Some also charge that it's just lazy wiring because soldering is more effective, it just takes longer to do. However, butt connectors and their similarly crimped fitting friends have their place, and that just might be in your ride.

Wiring Switches

You need a way to activate your valves, whether they're in a manifold or on their own. To do so, use a switch. If you've never worked with one before, the idea is pretty simple.

Let's say that you have one corner that you want to lift. The switch you'll need is a single-pole, double-throw (SPDT) momentary switch. What does that mean? Well, the momentary part means that it's temporary. You pull the switch, and once you release the toggle, it returns to the middle, which deactivates the circuit. The single pole refers to the power that you're using to trigger the circuit, and there's just one of them on the switch. Finally, the double-throw part refers to the two outputs that you have on the switch (top and bottom).

If you hold an SPDT switch (also called a "three-prong" to those who have worked with hydraulics in the past) in profile so that the switch itself points to the right, you can best visualize how it functions. Now, hold the switch up. If you draw an invisible line down the length of the switch, you'll see that the line would connect to the bottom pole on the switch. What that means is that

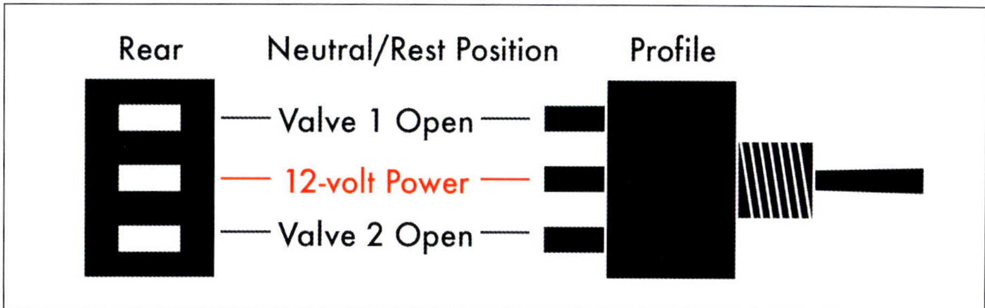

This is a single-pole, double-throw momentary switch in the rest position. At the center pole, there is power. The top pole holds the trigger for Valve 1, and the bottom pole holds the trigger for Valve 2.

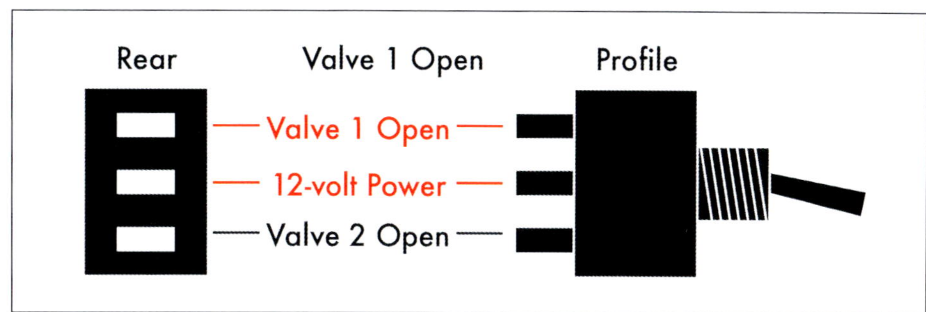

With the switch held down, the power from the center pole is now transferred to the top pole, which opens Valve 1.

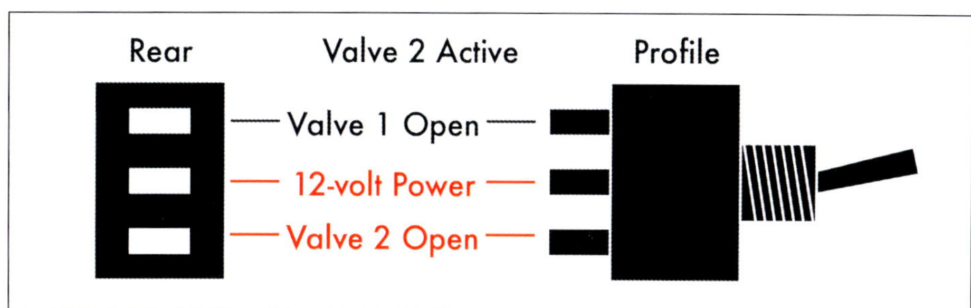

This is the same switch, but now the toggle is in the opposite direction, triggering Valve 2.

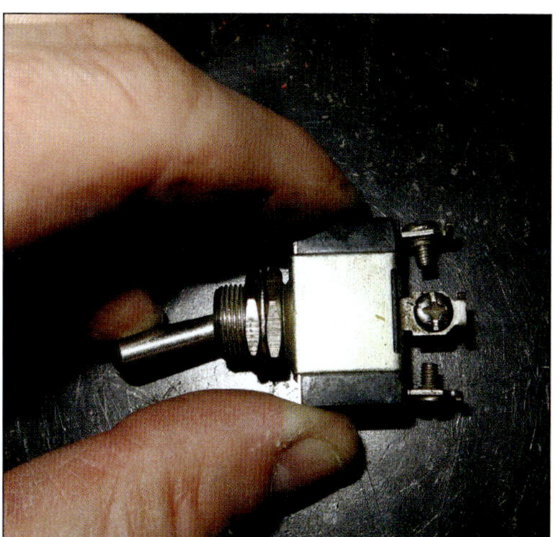

If you draw an imaginary line from the tip of the toggle to the end of the switch, it intersects with the pole on top of the body. That's the one that would receive power in this scenario.

Soldering Connections

If you want to make a professional connection between two wires that will be weather tight and strong, learn to solder. The process is similar to welding in that you're using a secondary material to bond two other metal pieces together. However, in this case, you finish everything off with a nice bit of heat-shrink tubing, which seals the connection tight. If done correctly, a soldered connection can last years.

Soldering can be tricky to learn and do, and if you're doing it upside down in the back of a car, it's even harder. However, once you get used to the system, it's really not bad, and you can do it anywhere.

Note: If you're doing this over something flammable like the carpet on the inside of your ride, put a piece of metal under the connection. It'll catch any stray splatter and keep things safe.

Various tools help you with this job. Clockwise from top is a wire stripper, another wire stripper, a soldering gun, a wet towel, assorted sizes of heat-shrink tubing, an adjustable helping hand, and solder.

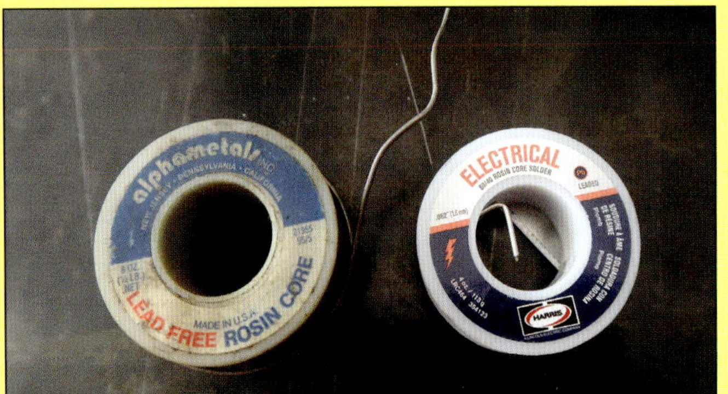

Let's start with the basics: you need solder to make your connections. There's lead-free solder (left) and lead solder. Either way, get some with a rosin core. That rosin acts as a flux for the solder itself and helps the process go smoother. If you have to choose between lead-free solder and lead solder, know that lead is known to be a cancer-causing agent, so if you have to use it, do so in an open environment with the proper protection.

Although the adjustable helping hand isn't critical, it certainly comes in handy. This way, you can hold both wires independently while using your hands to hold solder and the soldering gun. These are also made with magnetic bases for soldering in a vehicle.

1 *Start by stripping the wires down to an appropriate length. In this case, the installer is pretty liberal with the wire, as they have heat shrink to work with. The idea is that you want enough wire that once it is twisted with the other connection, it will make a strong mechanical bond.*

2 On the other side, slide the heat-shrink tubing over the end of the wire. If you forget this step, you'll be in a world of hurt later once the connection is made.

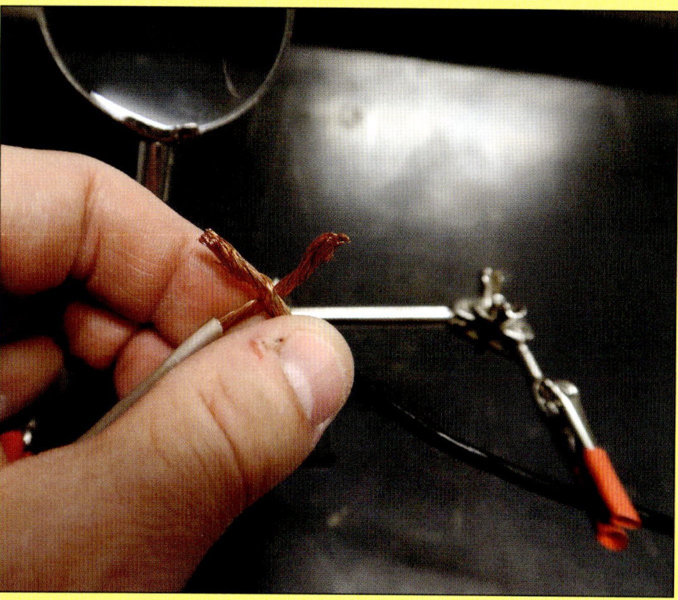

3 With the wires cut, stripped, and placed in the helping hand, be sure that the bare wire is tight. Then form an X with the connecting wire.

4 Now, twist the wires together tightly. If done correctly, there is a solid mechanical connection that can't be pulled apart easily. That's the goal.

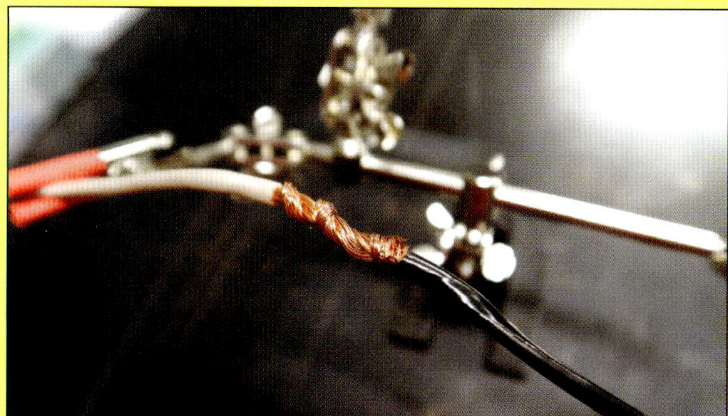

5 Plug in the soldering iron. After tinning the end (just dab some solder on the tip, then wipe it off on the damp towel), heat the wire. Don't touch the solder to the tip. Instead, the solder goes on the opposite side of the wire. The heat will then suck the solder into the joint, making a substantially stronger connection.

Soldering Connections *continued*

6 *Sometimes lead-free solder is difficult to work with and takes a while to heat. You can use additional flux on the joint, which can help speed up that process. If you do so, make sure it's approved for electrical connections, as plumbing flux and solder flux are two different things.*

7 *If you can still see strands of wire in the connection but they're now the color of solder, then you're doing well. Again, the solder should flow into the connection. Once you think you've done enough, try tugging on both ends. If you did it correctly, it'll stay rock solid.*

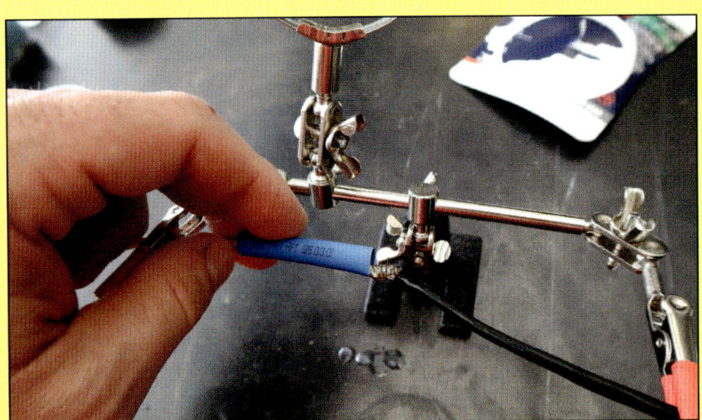

8 *Slide the heat-shrink tubing over the connection, making sure there's enough to go over both sides. Extend it past the existing shielding so that everything is tight.*

9 *Use anything from a heat gun to a lighter to heat the heat-shrink tubing. Just make sure that the heat is applied evenly across the connection.*

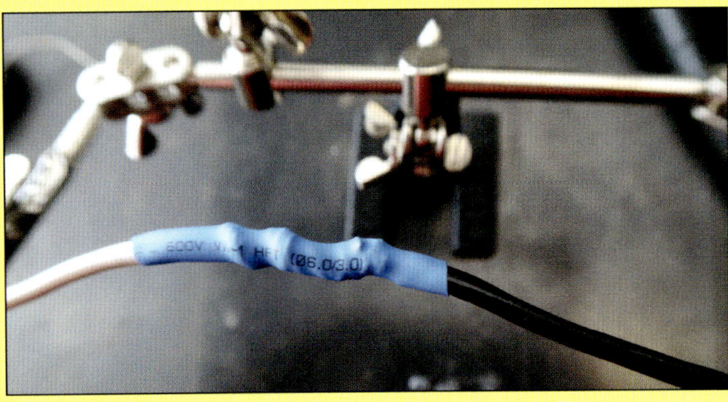

10 *The finished connection is now sealed tight and strong.*

The wiring here may look confusing, but it was carefully mapped out. Also, notice how the center pole on every switch is connected.

when you're lifting the switch up, you're putting power to the bottom pole. The same is true in reverse. If you push the switch down, power goes to the top pole.

Now, let's say you want to trigger two things at the same time. That's when you need a double-pole, double-throw (DPDT) switch, which is also called a "six-prong" switch. This is essentially two SPDT switches side by side. That means you have two potential power points and two things you can trigger each direction.

Next up is a three-pole, double-throw (3PDT) switch, which is also called a "nine-prong," and then a four-pole, double-throw (4PDT) switch, which is also called a "12-prong." Each of those just adds to the amount of things you can do.

Again, every version of these switches is a momentary, 12-volt DC switch.

In an airbag setup, there's no reason for you not to have a common power wire for each switch.

Therefore, most people just jump the 12-volt power lead from pole to pole, all the way across the middle of the switch panel. It's simple enough to do, and it makes the job easier. But what kind of switches do you need, and how do you wire them?

If you want to just lift the front and back of your truck, you need two DPDT switches. One pair of poles are wired to the two lift valves on the front or back, and the other pair goes to the drop valves. The middle poles are wired to 12-volt power.

However, chances are good that you want some kind of adjustability. Maybe you want to plan for scenarios where one side lifts higher than the other. If you want to lift and lower the front, back, left side, and right side, you need four DPDT switches wired the same at the front and back but pairing the sides on the other two switches.

What if you want individual corner adjustability? Then you want four SPDT switches: one wired for

each corner. What if you want front, back, left side, right side, and individual corners? That's eight switches total: four SPDTs and four DPDTs.

So, why would you ever need a 3PDT or a 4PDT?

In the world of hydraulics, dancing your vehicle is a thing. To do so, you want switches that do multiple things at the same time—a famous rapper once made a reference to 16 switches, after all. But one good reason for a 4PDT switch is what's called a pancake switch. It's where all your valves lift up or down simultaneously.

In practice, a pancake switch doesn't do very well lifting. Instead, you end up with a crooked vehicle. However, it's amazing for laying out your car or truck, and for that alone, you might want to consider wiring one.

Wiring Diagrams for Switch Panels

Putting together a switch panel can seem confusing at first. That's why these switch wiring diagrams are here: to make your life easier. In every case, the wiring follows a pattern: 1) front left corner lift valve, 2) front left corner dump valve, 3) front right corner lift valve, 4) front right corner dump valve, 5) rear left corner lift valve, 6) rear left corner dump valve, 7) rear right corner lift valve, 8) rear right corner dump valve, and 9) 12-volt power.

For reference, "left" is the driver's side of the vehicle in the US, and "right" is for the passenger's side. Pushing the switch up lifts the vehicle, while pushing it down lowers it. These diagrams are also viewed from the rear. That way, when you flip the panels over, everything is viewed normally.

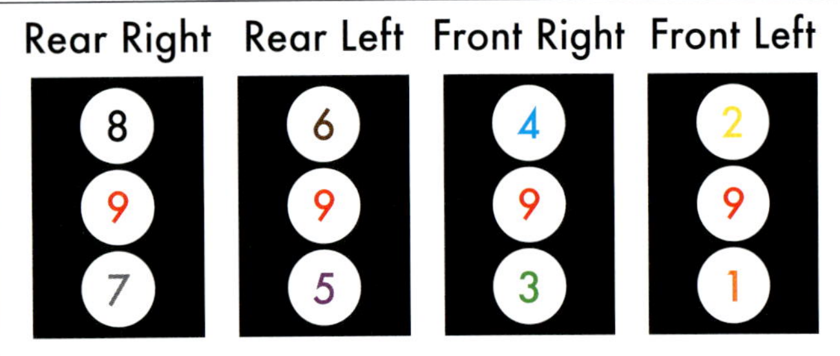

This is the simplest of switch panels because it just covers the four individual corners. That said, it's a nice panel to have if you want to make minute adjustments.

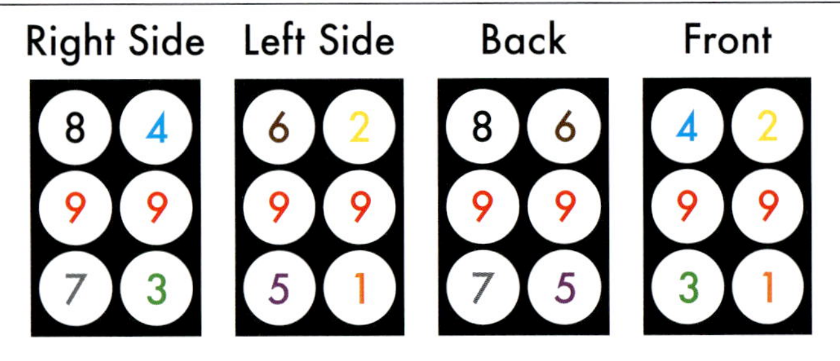

This front, back, left-side, right-side (FBSS) panel is arguably the most common. It's a simple way to go up and down every day, and, if need be, adjust a side. You can even show off a little if you like.

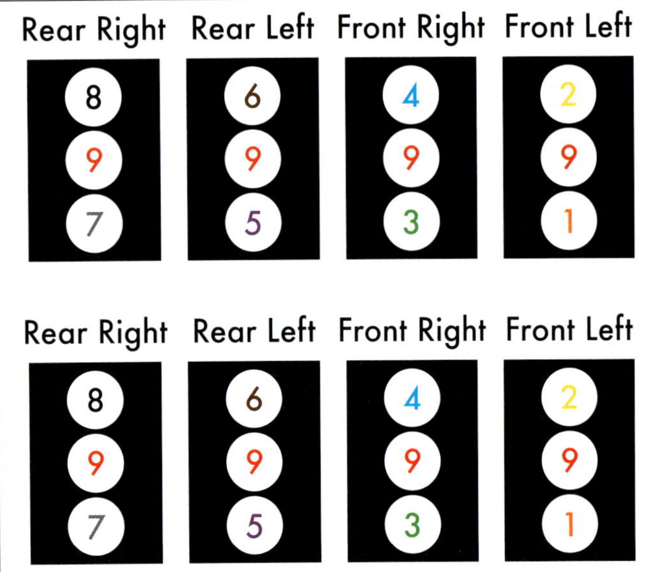

An eight-switch panel such as this is great because it lets you go up and down every day with the basic front and back switches, but it provides the precise control as well.

Wire Harnesses and Cables

Once you have the switch panel wired together, you need a way to get those signals to the respective valves. For that, you can either use a cable or a harness.

Cables come in all shapes and sizes, but what you want is a 9-wire cable. That means that you have nine wires carried inside of a single sheath. You'll need one wire for the lift valve on each corner, one for the dump valve on each corner, and one for 12-volt power. If you're wiring your own switch box, panel, or switches, this is the first choice.

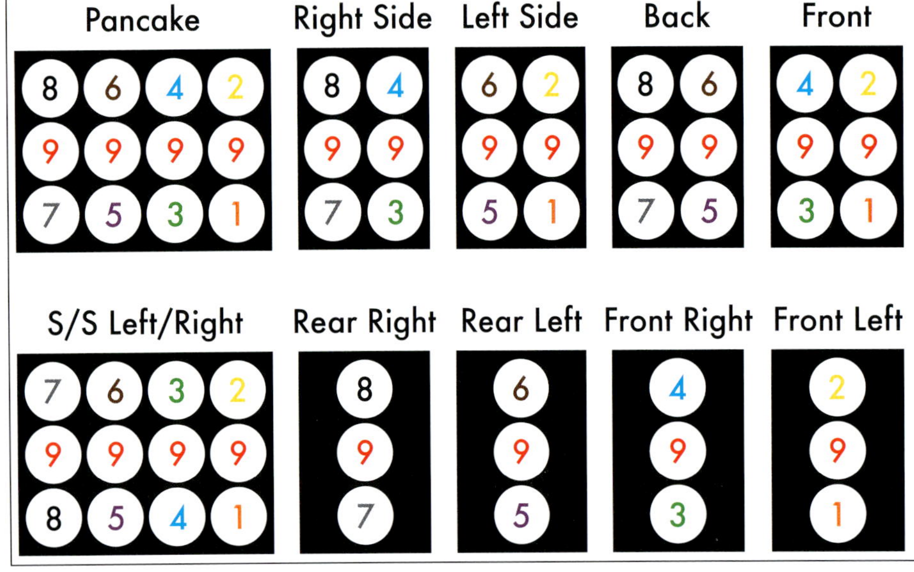

This 10-switch panel is fairly common too. It provides all the flexibility of an 8-switch panel but throws in pancake as well. The "S/S" stands for seesaw, which is when one side, the corner, or the end lifts while the opposite drops.

An option for keeping your wiring organized is a bus bar, which is also called a terminal block. If you use ring or spade terminals on your connections, you can screw them in on each end. It makes organizing the valves a lot easier.

Wire harnesses are usually valve and controller specific. For example, AVS makes a harness that connects one of its switch boxes with an Accu-Air valve setup. The nice thing about a harness is that everything plugs in place, so you don't have to think about whether or not you screwed something up in the wiring process. However, they're a little bit more expensive, so consider that too.

Switch Box and Panel Locations

With all of these switches, where do you put them all? Well, anywhere you want, really. The dashboard is a popular choice, and if there is a center console, that's a good location. Otherwise, you can just build something custom and make it work for you.

In the past, people bought electronics project boxes from Radio Shack. These had metal plates that screwed into a plastic package, and they were perfect for building a switch box. You'd lay out your switches onto the metal, drill them out, install your switches, and wire them up. Just run a nine-strand wire out the side, and you're ready to go.

Another popular option used to be making your own switch panels. These are pieces of aluminum that you drill out to mount your switches. Sometimes they had a 90-degree bend on one end with mounting screws so that you could secure them to the bottom of a dashboard.

Of course, there are other options.

Pre-Wired Switch Boxes

Today, there are two routes that most people choose. The first option is a pre-wired switch box. AVS sells a wide variety of them, as does Slam Specialties and several other companies. Sometimes these are built with traditional toggle switches, sometimes they are built with rocker switches, and other times they are built with manual valves. In each instance, you pick the number of switches, and there's probably a panel out there for you.

Digital Air Management

This is the second option, which is (in today's market) the most popular one.

AccuAir has the E-Level+, Ridetech has the RidePro-X, and AirLift has the 3H/3P. Each of these are height and/or pressure-adjusting leveling systems, and all of them come with (or have the ability to add) some kind of proprietary controller. Sometimes it's wired, sometimes it's Bluetooth capable, and sometimes it's a phone app—and some systems have all three.

In recent years digital air management systems have dominated the market. As a result, their controllers are all over the place. It also means that there's not a lot of wiring to do anymore, aside from plugging in a harness to your system's specific

This is an old switch panel wired up to do individual corners plus the front, back, left side, and right side.

The black square in the open cup holder is an AccuAir E-Level controller. It's one of the more popular ways to lift a car or truck.

setup. It's a lot easier and a lot less hands-on than in previous years.

So, why is this section all about wiring, when it's not as common as it used to be?

First off, everyone begins their airbag journey in a different place, and that may be with two SPDT switches and a dream. Automatic leveling systems are expensive, and it's not an easy entry point for many people. Plus, even if you have one, it never hurts to know how to wire these switches. Maybe you'll want four in your dash just for kicks.

The point is that it's good to know how everything works. That way, you'll know where to go if there's a problem.

Valve Manifolds

Then, there are valve manifolds, which are by far the more popular option as of this writing. These are blocks of aluminum that have been machined to hold multiple valve bodies. Sometimes the valves' wiring has been consolidated to work into one harness, while others still have individual wiring to wrangle. Either way, they all have inputs and outputs for air, and individual ports for each corner. A four-valve manifold controls two corners, while an eight-valve manifold controls four corners.

There are many reasons why this is the superior way to go. Manifolds are all one piece, so there are minimal fittings to work with. Therefore,

This is a VU4 manifold by AccuAir, and it's able to handle four individual corners. The gray plug at the top is there to connect a dedicated harness to it and make the install that much easier.

There are multiple ports on each manifold, but these (labelled 1, 2, 3, and 4) go to the airbag on each corner of the vehicle.

with less fittings, there is less potential for leaks (and less cost). You can buy the VU4 from Hornblasters.com or Switch Suspension for $395. AVS sells a set of eight of its fast valves for $600 with fittings. Which seems like a better deal to you? This is why manifolds have taken off in recent years. They're smaller, more efficient, easier to install, and cheaper too.

So, should you do a manifold on your setup? Yeah, probably. They're the best option on the market today, and they make the wiring process a lot smoother.

GAUGES

The best way to visualize the health and status of an air suspension system is with gauges. They're made to display the pressure in the system, and they come in many variations. There are single-needle gauges that show the pressure in one airbag or tank and dual-needle gauges that usually show a pair of airbags. There are also digital gauges, which display the same things but in a digital format, including all four corners and sometimes even the tank pressure.

The idea here is that you should have a way to know at a glance how much air is in one component at a time. It used to be common to find guys with three gauges mounted somewhere in their vehicle: one dual-needle gauge for the front bags; one dual-needle gauge for the rear airbags; and one single-needle gauge for the tanks. With a setup like this, you could lift your vehicle to your favorite pressure and know if your tank was running low on air.

In the early days of airbags, gauges were almost a requirement. Today? Well, thanks to the rise of digital air management systems, they're not quite as popular, although they're still a handy tool. Instead of mounting them to a pil-lar pod for display, they're often put into the glove box or otherwise hidden. Also, some digital air management systems include their own gauges, which are integrated into their controllers or apps. This makes traditional gauges unnecessary, unless you want something more analog for style or specificity.

Ultimately, it depends on the user. If you like knowing the pressure or don't plan on running a digital air management system, you should have gauges. Even if you do have a 3H kit or something similar in the works, at a minimum, you should have a tank pressure gauge even if it's just mounted on the tank itself.

The air tank holds air that your airbag suspension needs to lift, so it's obviously a pretty important part of the system. It's also handy if you have a problem with your setup. Say that your compressors never seem to

The gauges on this 1973–1980 Chevy truck are tucked into the factory bezel, replacing what were two dead spots in the panel. It's a clean way to hide your gauges in plain sight.

shut off. Is it the pressure switch, a leak in your tank, or do you just have too little capacity to run the system to your liking? If you have a gauge on the tank, you can determine the answer. If the pressure switch goes bad, the tank gauge will read a pressure above what the switch turns off at. If the tank is leaking, you'll never trip that switch and never turn off the compressors. If you have a small tank (or a really high demand on the system), the gauge will display that as well. It's not a perfect system, but it's an analog way to help narrow down options when you're troubleshooting.

So, now you know the basics of what gauges are with your setup, plus when and where to use them. Now, let's talk about the different types.

If you want gauges integrated into your airbag setup, you need to decide if you want an analog gauge (also called a mechanical gauge) or a digital one. The difference, ultimately, comes down to how the gauge gets its signal.

Analog/Mechanical

Analog gauges are mechanical in nature. This means that the material (in this case, air) is physically delivered to the gauge via an air line, where it displays the type of reading that is requested. For example, mechanical oil pressure gauges have a small hose with oil that runs to the back of the device. Air gauges function the same way but have air flowing to them instead.

This means that if you want to get the pressure of a particular component (an airbag, the tank, a pair of airbags, etc.), a physical line is needed that runs from that item into the interior of your vehicle and then to the back of the gauge. Although this sounds difficult to do, it's not bad. You don't need a large-diameter line to do it; 1/8-inch soft line will work just fine. It's small enough to run through corners, under carpet, or in a pillar, so it's not a big deal.

It gets more complex when you add more lines, and it varies based on where everything is mounted. For example, one common gauge mounting spot is on the A-pillar, with a three-gauge pod. Autometer sells replacement A-pillars with that setup for around $80 depending on your vehicle.

If you're running three gauges and have two dual-needle gauges and a single-needle gauge, you have five 1/8-inch air lines running through your dash and up into the pillar. That's not a lot of space, and it can get frustrating at times to get everything situated. Plus, there's the issue of making sure the lines don't get pinched along the way. Otherwise, you won't get the air at all.

Of course, there is a solution for that: change what kind of gauge is used.

Digital

If you want to avoid running air line into the cabin of the vehicle, the next choice is to go digital. A digital gauge doesn't use a mechanical

This particular truck had a custom center console made of medium-density fiberboard (MDF) and fiberglass. The owner built these pods for his analog air pressure gauges and angled them toward the driver.

On this 1951 Ford, the gauge panel is tucked under the dashboard so that it doesn't ruin the aesthetics.

In this case, the user has two Dakota Digital gauges: one that reads tank pressure and another that shows all four corner pressures of his airbag setup.

means to get its signal. Instead, it has a sending unit. This sending unit threads into the area where you want to pull the signal. Then, run wires from it to the gauge.

There are many options for digital gauges. Dakota Digital is one of the gold standards, but there's also GlowShift Gauges, AVS, and Bag Riders. They all do the same basic thing with a sending unit and a gauge that receives the signal. If you're looking for a clean and simple way to display and run the gauges, digital is a good option.

Mounting Options

The nice thing about air gauges is that they come in a wide variety of sizes (both analog and digital) and are pretty easy to mount. Because of that, you can get pretty creative with how they're placed.

The most common placement (probably because it's the easiest and quite affordable) is a simple gauge pod. These either mount to the existing A-pillar panel (or replace it entirely) and can contain multiple types and sizes of gauges. You can also use individual pods that you mount wherever you like or build something custom in a center console or your dash.

All of this couldn't be easier. Pick your diameter of gauge, get a matching mounting cup or plate, and you're off to the races. Get as creative as you want. Your only limitation is how to get your wiring or air lines to the gauges. Otherwise, have at it.

This 1998 Chevrolet Silverado had a single Dakota Digital gauge mounted on a single pod molded into the steering column cover. It shows the bag pressure in all four corners and, once you push the button, the tank pressure.

Do You Need Gauges?

This is, of course, a loaded question. In the airbag world, there are plenty of people who love having gauges. It's a way to show the health and activity of your system and a physical representation of what's going on. Just like a tachometer is good for knowing your engine's RPM, an air pressure gauge is good for your airbags, right?

The thing is that air pressure isn't actually the best way to measure how the bags are doing. That's because pressure can fluctuate a lot based on temperature, barometric pressure, or weight from a ladder in the bed of your truck or the burrito you ate. Even just driving will cause your bag pressure gauges to bounce around, and the longer the length of the line running to the gauge affects how much they shift.

So, what is the best option? In today's market, it's stepping up to a digital air management system of some kind. There are both pressure-based and height-based options, and they each have their pros and cons. However, when the vehicle does all the heavy lifting, you don't really need to know exactly what each corner is doing.

To answer the question, no, you really don't need gauges. However, if you like knowing what's going on, there's no reason not to add them if you like. It's dealer's choice, so feel free to go out there and do what makes you feel more secure. ∎

The billet panel just below the climate controls is an older-style digital gauge that shows all four corners plus the tank.

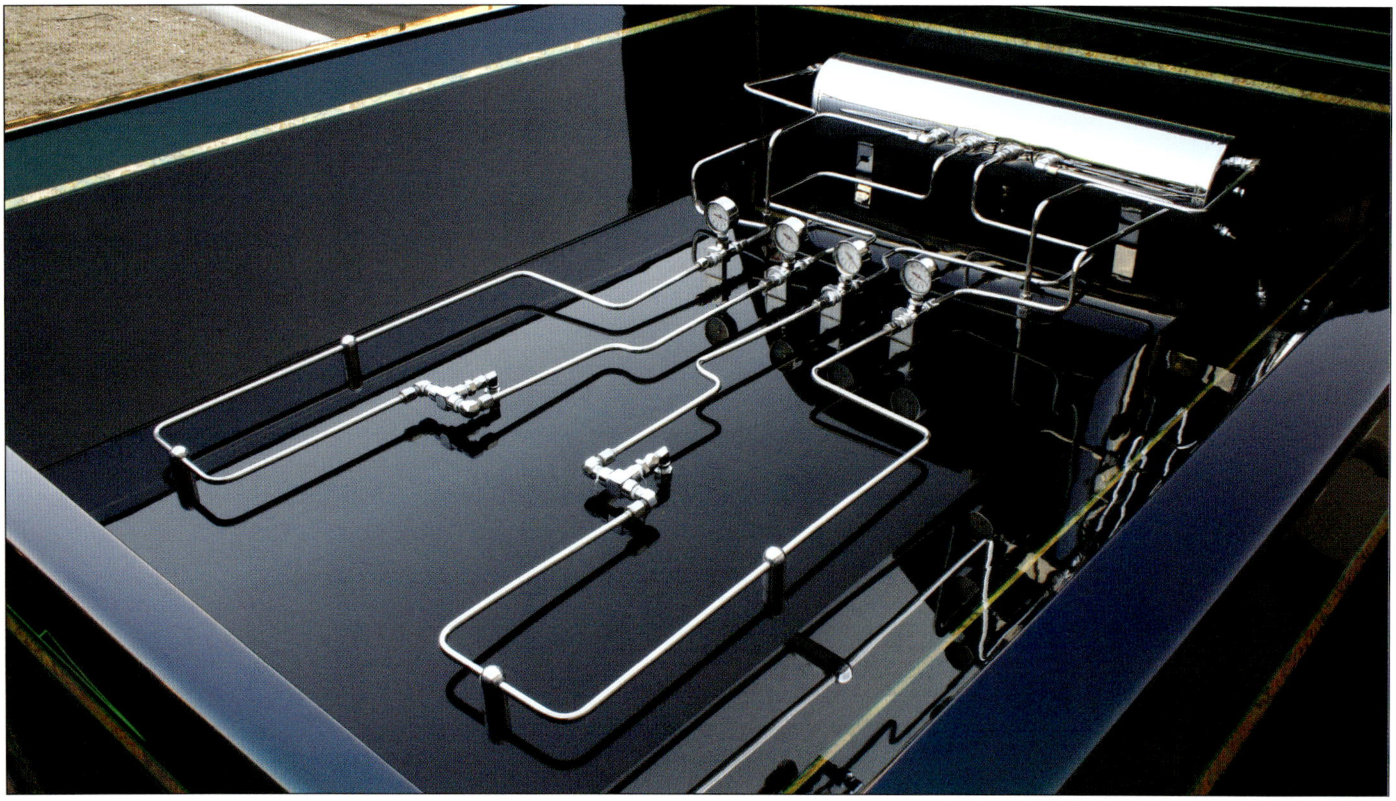

Want to get really creative? The builder of this truck had a background in classic lowriders and wanted a way to show that off. Chromed hard line and analog gauges in the bed are a great way to do just that.

     HOW TO INSTALL AIR RIDE SUSPENSION SYSTEMS

WHAT IS AN AIRBAG?

This may seem like an odd question to bring up in Chapter 7. However, at the end of the day, what is an airbag at its core?

An airbag is actually an air spring. Although that may sound like semantics, it's an important aspect to note. For one, many people think of airbags like the ones found in your car for safety, but that's not even close to the same design that is used for suspensions. Instead, for this application, you're looking at a pneumatic device that is typically built with a bellows design (but not always) and uses air and rubber to support the vehicle instead of a metal spring.

Now, a traditional metal spring has what's called a spring rate. That's defined as how much weight it takes to compress a spring 1 inch. Let's put that into context.

Say that you have a regular coil spring in the back of your truck mounted on the axle and frame just like they did way back in the day, and it has a 400-pound spring rate. That means for every 400 pounds that is placed in the truck bed, the coil spring compresses 1 inch. Add another 400 pounds, and the truck's rear end sinks another inch, bringing the total weight on the suspension to 800 pounds. However, here's the thing: the spring rate is still the same (at 400 pounds).

Now, swap that coil out for an airbag. It can still do the job and handle the same amount of weight (depending on the bag). However, because it can be inflated and deflated to adjust its height, it has a variable spring rate. The more it's compressed, the higher the spring rate will be. That's why you can take two identical airbags at the same PSI and put them in two different vehicles and find different spring rates in each.

In this way, an airbag is very similar to a progressive-rate spring. They also see an increased spring rate whenever they're compressed further, which helps when you're slamming your car into a turn. As a result, the same applies with a properly set up airbag system.

Airbag Types

Airbags come in a lot of different shapes and sizes, but primarily you'll deal with them in two forms: bellows and sleeves.

This is a sleeve-style bag. These are typically found in the rear of a vehicle, whether it's for load-leveling purposes on a truck or a smooth ride on a hot rod.

This is a Slam Specialties airbag being prepped for installation. Airbags come in various shapes and sizes, and it's important that you find the best fit for your vehicle.

Selection for Specific Applications

This is where things get both interesting and wonky. A quick bit of googling shows what kind of airbags various people use in their own installs, and that will provide a solid starting point. However, let's go through it.

Say that you want to put airbags on your 1978 Chevrolet Silverado. RideTech sells 224C airbags for its kit, while Slam Specialties offers the HE-7, which is a direct replacement for the 224C and Firestone's 2600 airbag. With all that information, you can deduce that you want a 7-inch bag, which will work well in that truck.

However, what if you're bagging an application that's never (or rarely) been bagged before? In that case, you're moving into unknown territory, so you need to take some measurements. One thing that some people do is get some pipe that's the same diameter as the airbag they want to install. Then, they put it in the place where the airbag would go to see if it fits. Try that yourself on a project. If it fits, you're good. If not,

try again with another size. You'll get it eventually.

Convoluted Airbags

Convoluted airbags, also known as bellows, are considered to be the default airbag by most builders. That's probably because for many years it was the only option. Early customizers started with Firestone's

line of bags, and the automotive customization industry used them as a starting point too. That's why many companies refer to their sizes based on Firestone's existing models.

What makes them so special? Well, they're a double convoluted bag, which means that they have a band in the middle that gives them their unique shape. They're fairly affordable and can be used in more applications than a sleeve or strut bag. They also can handle a wide range of weights, so you can bag everything from a mid-1980s Toyota pickup to a Ford F-350 crew cab dually and larger.

This brings us to lifting capacity. A Slam Specialties SS-5 is a 5½-inch-diameter bag that gets almost 6 inches of lift. The SS-8 is an 8-inch-diameter bag that gets a little over 10 inches of lift. Both get more lift than the average sleeve bag, and they both have different capacities. Not everything fits in the right space, but if there is room, which one would you choose?

The location of the bag matters too. In this scenario, the airbag has a 1:1 lift ratio, which means that it needs lower air pressure to ride smoother. Were the bag on a link-bar system of some kind, that would change.

The airbags on the rear of this 1972 Chevrolet Blazer frame use a KP Components cantilever kit. This puts more pressure on the airbag, gives the user more lift, and rides smooth too.

Finally, think about ride quality. The heavier the vehicle, the heavier capacity you need for the bag, right? Sure. However, you also want to consider that the heavy-duty airbag might be too stiff to be functional. So, going with an airbag that has the correct capacity for your build but isn't going overboard is also key. In this scenario, sleeve airbags often hold the advantage, as they ride quite smoothly. However, since they don't have as many flexible mounting options (and can't lift as much weight), convoluted wins the race.

As a result, you'll often see convoluted airbags in many installs. It's the most common application out there, and it works well for most scenarios.

Sleeve Airbags

Sleeve airbags also come in various shapes and forms, but the basic idea is that it's a sleeve of rubber that's sometimes wider at the top than at the bottom. These provide a super-soft ride but often at the expense of a few things.

First, it's the weight capacity of the airbag. A Firestone 224 (a very popular model of convoluted airbag) can hold 3,400 pounds at 150 psi. Then, there's their Ridetech sleeve spring, which will hold 1,500 pounds at 100 psi. The Firestone bag has almost 6 inches of lift, while the Ridetech sleeve gets 7½ inches. It sounds like the Ridetech sleeve should win, right? However, in the end, the Firestone almost always takes the cake because of not only the capacity but also its mounting flexibility.

As a result, you'll often see sleeve airbags in two applications: on the

This 1959 Suburban has a pair of sleeve airbags out back that are seen hanging from the crossmember. They give the rear end of the SUV a great ride, and since lift isn't a huge priority, they get the job done. (Photo Courtesy Switch Suspension)

Port Sizes and Airbags

Every airbag needs a way to get air in, and that's through the port. It's typically (but not always) located on the top of the bag. It comes in various NPT thread sizes and sometimes even has the fitting preinstalled. So, does that port size matter? Absolutely.

As mentioned previously, the slowest part of your airbag setup is the smallest component in the system, and that dictates the overall speed. You could have 1-inch fittings running everywhere, but if there is a 1/4-inch port going into the airbag, it slows down the entire system.

Again, speed isn't always important. However, if you're buying airbags, it never hurts to go up a size if you're not sure. You can always run a smaller air line fitting into the bag and then upgrade if it's too slow. Just make sure to factor in the port size before buying the bags because that's not something you can cheaply fix later. ◼

rear of a car or truck where it won't see a ton of additional weight or as a helper airbag to assist otherwise-stock trucks with extra load capacity.

This is not meant to diminish the role of a sleeve airbag. Its place in the system is still quite positive, and when they're put in the back of a vehicle, they can be heavenly to cruise with. However, most people stick with one type of bag, and that's usually a convoluted/bellows model.

Strut Bags

Back when airbags first became a thing, the guys and girls with Hondas (which were very popular in the late 1990s) looked at bags with lust in their eyes. Their cars had struts, and there was no easy way to make a strut work with an airbag. By design, the strut itself had to go through the airbag, which wouldn't let it hold air. Many people tried to make this design work and failed, and although the resulting creations were pretty crazy (for example: airbags mounted on upper control arms and then sticking out through the hood), it wasn't their time.

Now, you can buy strut bags right off the shelf for a wide variety of cars. Those same Honda Civic guys have many options that are all made for their specific vehicle.

That's the thing about strut bags:

This is a strut bag installed on a Volkswagen Atlas. The threaded shaft allows the owner to fine tune the ride height even further. (Photo Courtesy Switch Suspension)

they're vehicle specific. You can't just buy any old set and make them work on any vehicle. The manufacturers of these kits pick the right bags and mounts for each car. That way, they perform the best.

In addition, some of these setups are built like coilovers. They have adjustable mounts and a threaded strut body that allows you to tune how high or low you want the bag to sit. That's a great option because

This is a strut bag in a Dodge Charger Hellcat. It bolts right into the factory strut tower and the steering knuckle. Notice that there's a flexible hose coming out the bottom. That's the air line, and it's made of stainless steel to handle extra abuse. (Photo Courtesy Lonnie Thompson)

not everyone wants the car to lay on the ground. Strut bag manufacturers know that some people want the convenience of height adjustability but still want to be able to drive laid out and accommodate them accordingly.

What's the downside? Well, it's often not cheap to get a kit. Some are upward of $2,400, and although that includes the airbags and struts for all four corners, it's a steep entry price point for many people. Of course, it's completely dependent on the car that you own and whether or not they're necessary. If it's not necessary and you can go with traditional airbags, you'll have a cheaper way to go.

There are many airbags on this shelf in various sizes. Make sure to get the right one for your build. (Photo Courtesy Switch Suspension)

Various-Diameter Airbags

Just like every airbag has a different capacity, they also have various diameters too. The diameter for the bag you choose often dictates how it's installed and what kind of lift you end up getting.

That's because larger-diameter airbags tend to get more lift than

Adjustable Spring Rates and Spring Loads

If you were shopping for lowering springs for your vehicle today, you'd find an abundance of information about spring rates. Airbags also have a spring rate, but it's adjustable. So, what does all that mean?

Let's recap a few things. At its core, a spring rate is the amount of force it takes to make a spring travel 1 inch of distance. However, let's turn this into an analogy for clarity. Say that you want to buy a trampoline. If you put a child on it that weighs 50 pounds and they can make the trampoline sink 1 inch every time they stand on it, that's a soft trampoline. If you put a 400-pound man on another trampoline and it only sinks 1 inch, it's a very firm trampoline; the child would barely make it move. That's essentially how spring rate works. The kid's trampoline has a spring rate of 50 pounds, while the other one has a spring rate of 400 pounds. This is how you measure how soft or firm a spring is.

Now, let's talk about spring loads. This is the amount of weight a spring can carry at a specific height. Let's go back to the trampoline idea. Say that you build trampolines, and you want one where it will deflect 1¾ inches when a 200-pound man stands in the middle. You can do that with the right engineering and design, and that's how a spring load works. This is more about the engineering behind the process, not a measure of its softness.

What does all this have to do with airbags? Well, airbags have an adjustable spring rate. As the people at Ridetech put it, the more you compress an air spring, the higher your spring rate is.

In this way, airbags can be an advantage for the daily driver who wants to have a car that still handles well. Driving straight down the road, the spring rate stays soft, providing a comfortable ride. However, when you turn, there's more pressure on the corner, and it compresses the air spring, thus raising the spring rate and providing a firmer ride.

In addition, you can put the same airbag with the same pressure at the same place on the chassis in two different vehicles, and you'll have different spring rates in each.

Another point to note is that some builders use leverage to get more lift on a setup, doing what's called a "cantilever" installation. This also affects the spring rate, so consider that when you select the bags and factor in how much they can safely support.

As you build the system, someone will inevitably point out that you're making something with an adjustable spring rate, and that makes it inherently unsafe. Here's your ammunition against that argument. ■

---

their smaller counterparts (no real surprise there). However, there's also a tipping point because a bag that's too small won't be able to carry the weight you need. For example, if you're looking to bag the front end of a 1977 Chevrolet Silverado with an inline-6 under the hood, you can get away with a bag on the smaller side. However, if you have a big-block under the hood, that won't be the case. Make sure that you have enough capacity on hand. Otherwise, the bags will fail.

As a result, there are many things to consider when selecting an airbag, and diameter is just one of them. Know that every airbag you look at will have different dimensions, and unless the manufacturer specifically says that they're designed to replace X model, you need to verify that they'll work in your application.

Installation Requirements

You have the basics of airbags down by now, but where can you install them? There are a few different scenarios, but one basic requirement comes into play: if you're replacing a coil spring, you can probably install an airbag in its place.

Why is that? Think about the location where springs typically sit. They're between the control arm and the frame of a car or truck. The spring is mounted on a piece that moves, and therefore, has a pivot. The spring is not placed between two objects and asked to keep the load centered or stable on its own. Instead, it usually has one solid mounting point paired with a pivot, which provides the stability and flexibility that is required.

The next factor is clearance. You need enough space around the air-

In this case, the part that's stable is the frame, while the part that pivots is the axle (specifically on the leaf spring mounts). (Photo Courtesy Switch Suspension)

To get extra clearance around the bag, the team at Switch Suspension cut out some of the frame on the factory spring pocket on this 1950 Cadillac. (Photo Courtesy Switch Suspension)

bag so that when it's inflated it won't rub against anything. Keep that last word in mind because it's critical. Anything that rubs against the airbag can eventually wear a hole in it or cause problems, so make sure that you don't let that happen. This is where the airbag's diameter comes into play.

If there is metal in the way, grind it down or cut it for clearance. If there is a brake line nearby, relocate it. Whatever you need to do to keep the airbag free of any contact is the goal. Also, make sure that it works at all points of travel from deflated to inflated to halfway up and everywhere in between.

We've already addressed capacity, and that's another option to consider. The airbag you install must be able to carry the load that it's under. Make sure that you exceed those stated rates at least by a little to keep yourself safe.

To ensure that there was clearance out back, a piece of steel pipe was used as a mockup for a compressed airbag. This way, they could make sure that nothing would be in their way before anything is welded. (Photo Courtesy Switch Suspension)

Airbags and Performance

There's this rumor that goes around some automotive circles, and it's pretty straightforward: if you have airbags, you don't have a performance vehicle. That may have been true 20 years ago, but today it's absolutely not the case.

There are many manufacturers that build airbag components designed for high-performance cars and trucks. One of them is Air Lift Performance, which has been in the air scene for decades. Its Performance Series struts have full air adjustability but totally tunable shock absorption, which makes them perfect for the street or the track. They even add 3 inches of height adjustability to the strut body so that you can go from fully slammed to just low enough with a twist of a knob—and they're not the only company doing that.

You can find performance shocks too, making any airbag setup handle that much better. Combine that with better sway bars, bushings, and other suspension components, and your bagged ride can handle the twisty roads with the best of them.

If you're looking for that kind of experience with your build, take some time and research what kind of companies offer products for your ride. Know that even though height adjustability is a big part of your performance journey, it doesn't have to put on the brakes. ■

DIGITAL AIR MANAGEMENT SYSTEMS

If there's one thing that has completely revolutionized the airbag industry in the past decade, it's the introduction of reliable digital air management systems for the mass market. The idea is pretty straightforward: you, as the owner of an airbagged vehicle, probably lift it to approximately the same height every day with a few variations. Possibly, you lift the front to give the tires clearance around corners, or maybe you have a pair of heights where you like to cruise. Generally, you're always lifting and lowering to the same positions.

A digital air management system does that exact task for you. Just get in your ride, turn the key, and either the airbags lift up automatically to a predetermined setting or you're just a button press away from getting there. It takes one of the friction points out of airbag ownership, and it looks super cool too.

It took a long time to get to this point. In the 1990s and early 2000s, there were digital air management systems that either weren't reliable or didn't work well, and when paired with their cost, they just weren't popular. It was baffling that it took so long to turn into reality. Busses have long had load leveling systems in place, and modern cars have similar systems too. Why couldn't the aftermarket figure it out?

Well, it did, and when that happened, everything changed. Now, they're the standard and not the aspirational norm. Customers come into shops speaking the name brand of the digital air management system instead of saying, "I want airbags." Because they're so user friendly, it's expanded the market to those who aren't as mechanically inclined as their car-loving friends. It's a pretty great solution.

So, how do they work and what do they do? Today, digital air management systems break down into two primary camps: pressure-based systems and height-sensor based systems. The differences between the two are vast.

Pressure-Based Systems

Let's play with a hypothetical. You have a 2010 Ford F-150 on

The RidePro X by Ridetech is a digital air management system. By utilizing its components, you can automatically raise and lower your vehicle to preset heights. (Photo Courtesy Jim Pickering)

airbags. You have an air valve manifold, four switches in the dash, and two compressors. There's a trio of gauges in your pillars and everything is functioning reliably, but you want to make it run a bit smoother and automatically. That's when you decide to get a pressure-based digital air management system.

The idea is that you're already familiar with the pressures that your truck typically runs. Your F-150 could need 100 psi up front and 60 psi out back to ride smooth. Maybe you have an even more finely tuned sense of where things go, and you know that you like to have 125 psi on the driver-side front and 107 psi on the passenger-side front. So, if you programmed in your pressure-based system with those numbers, you'd be able to just get in and go. It's the solution you've been looking for.

For many people, it is. These setups allow you to automatically set the pressures you want in your airbag system and give you presets to trigger them. It's a pretty convenient setup.

However, it also has drawbacks.

Pros and Cons

Say that you have one of these pressure-based systems in your F-150 when you get a call from your buddy. He's moving, and he needs some help transporting a couch. You have a truck, and the bed is free since you have everything air related mounted underneath. So, you figure that it's no big deal. You drive the truck over, load up the couch, and get ready to go.

However, now when you hit the preset to lift to your pre-determined height, you're stuck. You need more pressure to lift the back because you have all that extra weight from the couch. You can manually adjust things to make it work, but isn't the

point of these things to not have to do that?

Take the same truck but in a different scenario. It's the autumn, and temperatures are dropping. You go to lift the truck, and it's riding lower than usual. Well sure, of course it is. Pressures fluctuate based on temperature and atmospheric conditions, so 60 psi in the back bags on Tuesday may not be the same as on Wednesday.

Finally, this is the most basic scenario: you decide to bring a friend to the store. Their weight on the passenger's side of the vehicle will alter whether or not the truck is sitting level. Therefore, you sit crooked until they get out. It's not like you can plan for this situation by putting in a preset for passengers; your significant other could weigh more or less than your friend, and you probably have buddies at all sorts of different sizes.

So, why would you go with this kind of system when it seems as if there are so many flaws?

First, some people like gauges. They want to know exactly how well (or not) the air setup is working at all times, and gauges are the simplest way to show that. If you have a pressure-based system, those gauges are not only still valid but they're also a good way to diagnose or assess issues that come up. That gives them an edge.

Second, just because the pressure isn't always going to be constant, that doesn't make it a bad thing. It doesn't matter if it's pressure or height based. Most, if not all, digital air management systems have a way to adjust corners individually. Who cares about whether or not it's always 100-percent level, anyway?

Third, it's the ease of installation.

Height-based systems require special brackets and linkages to determine where your ride height is and uses that data to determine how your vehicle should sit. Those brackets are more complicated to install than just popping in an electronic control unit (ECU) and a few inline sensors like you'd get with a pressure-based system.

Finally, there's the cost. Height-based systems are more expensive than their pressure-based counterparts (usually by a few hundred dollars). That's enough for some people to lean that direction alone, and there's nothing wrong with that. If it does the job that you want it to do and it's cheaper, it's a win-win for you.

Digital air management systems are great no matter which way you cut it. Sure, pressure-based setups have their problems, but so do height-based ones. Nothing is perfect. If it gets you closer to where you want to be and automates the vehicle the way you want, it's a good thing.

Height-Sensor-Based Systems

Now you have a handle on how pressure-based systems work, but what about their brothers in air, the height-sensor-based systems? To explain it, let's revisit the example of the Ford F-150, full air ride setup with gauges and all. The upgrade to a height-sensor system is a little different.

To start, you need to install the sensors and ECU. Those sensors are small levers that can be mounted any number of ways, but the scenario is the same. The base of the sensor is mounted solid, and then there's an arm that's connected to a pivoting

Just forward of the tie rod on this frame is an AccuAir height sensor. The rod connects the lower control arm to the linkage and travels with the suspension, feeding the AccuAir ECU the data it needs to perform accurately.

joint. That arm has to rotate throughout the range of your suspension's motion, whether it's on the front or rear of the vehicle. Therefore, you have to mount one end of the joint to something that moves, such as the axle, leaf spring, lower control arm, or something similar.

The next part of the equation is the ECU, and this is what connects the sensors to your valves. You can run either the manufacturer's valves or not (some systems work as add-ons to what you already have), but the ECU does the heavy lifting. It uses either a proprietary controller or a smartphone app as an interface (possibly both). After a brief programming session, you can set a few presets, and you're ready to hit the road.

What's the day-to-day experience like? Some systems start right when you turn the key; the car or truck will lift to a predetermined ride height, and you're ready to go. If you want to drive higher or lower, either hit a preset height on the controller or app or just tap the up and down buttons. If you add a passenger or carry that friend's sofa home for him, the system automatically lifts or lowers the vehicle accordingly, so you don't even have to think about it. Everything is done automatically.

This system can't be perfect though, right? So far, it certainly sounds like it is. However, let's talk about the good and the bad.

Pros and Cons

There are quite a few positives with this kind of system. It can't be overstated enough that getting in your vehicle, turning the key (or pushing a button) to start it and watching your vehicle rise to a pre-determined height is pretty magical. To know that you'll always have an exact idea of where your car or truck is sitting thanks to your presets is also amazing.

The downside is the cost. These setups aren't cheap, and even though you can start out simple with a few add-ons to what you already have, the costs balloon quickly. The sticker shock can hit pretty hard, so don't take it lightly.

Installation isn't necessarily difficult, but properly setting up the height sensors isn't always fun. There may be tweaking and tuning to get

Here's the height sensor for the RidePro X by Ridetech. In this case, it mounts to the frame on one side and the axle on the other. As long as it can go through the full range of motion, it's good. (Photo Courtesy Jim Pickering)

things the way you want them, so keep that in mind. On the flip side, these kinds of systems are so popular that some aftermarket suspension companies work in mounts for sensors because they know their customers will use them. In those scenarios, installation usually goes pretty smooth.

Otherwise, you have the same problem with both types of setups in that you're now relying on a computer to establish your ride height. That's not a bad thing, but if a controller ever goes out or the ECU fails, it can be a real hassle. One could make the argument that similar problems happen with even simple systems, but still, it's something to think about.

Hybrid Systems

For the customer who wants a little bit of everything, there are hybrid systems on the market as well. Admittedly, there aren't many. However, the ones that are on the market combine the height sensors and pressure monitors to create a system that automatically sets the ride height

AccuAir

It's hard to talk about any digital air management system without referencing AccuAir. Although other companies had kits before this company, it took off in recent years and has become so popular that it was reaching "Kleenex" levels of ubiquity. AccuAir was the standard for these types of setups for years. Sure, it had competition, but you didn't see those kits out in the wild as often. AccuAir just had the edge.

Then COVID-19 happened, and just two weeks into the California lockdown, they closed up shop for good. Rumors abounded as to why. The company posted the following message on Instagram in an image:

"Dear customers and friends,

"With very heavy hearts, we must announce that AccuAir Suspension is permanently closed as of today. After 18 years or relentless blood, sweat, and tears, the COVID-19 pandemic has proven insurmountable for the business. The California closure that was expected to last only two weeks has now been extended through the end of April or possibly longer. Our dedicated team members and founders fought relentlessly, but a final decision from our investors forded this devastating outcome."

This was followed with the post copy:

"Words cannot express the gratitude that we have for the many customers who loyally supported AccuAir over the past 18 years and made it possible for us to create the most innovative products in the industry. Although the end is bitter, our role in making aftermarket air suspension grow from niche to mainstream was pretty sweet. The many families that our business provided for (both internal and external) and the many close relationships developed over all those years offers us some consolation that it wasn't 'all for nothing.' For those who have an open order or pending RMA, you'll be contacted by the bankruptcy court to resolve all creditor claims. Unfortunately, all operations have been stopped, and there is no staff to address your questions.

"We know that many other companies are facing similar challenges (or will be soon), and many jobs have already been lost. We wish the very best to all of you during this unprecedented time."

This was a huge deal to the aftermarket world. It was to the point that most airbagged vehicles had AccuAir suspension, and just a few months prior at SEMA, the company introduced the new and improved e-Level+ system. Plus, there was no talk of another company buying out patents or anything similar. It was just a quick shutdown.

What's worse is that some AccuAir owners relied on the smartphone app to operate their suspensions. Now, without anyone to update their apps, they were stuck—potentially literally.

Then, something happened.

A company named Arnott Industries purchased AccuAir's assets in late 2020. The company stated the following on its website answering the question, "Is AccuAir back?"

"The short answer is sort of. Arnott, LLC purchased the assets of AccuAir out of the bankruptcy and will be reviving the brand as a new company with a mix of classic and new products. We expect to relaunch the brand and products in 2021. So, while some of the AccuAir products are returning, AccuAir will be returning as a new company in a new location with new staff. Arnott's long history (more than 30 years) of engineering and manufacturing replacement OEM air suspension systems for cars and motorcycles is a great fit with the AccuAir brand and product."

To date, the brand has started to come back out onto the market, and there are signs of a revival. However, the company took a big hit to its reputation with the quick shutdown. Time will tell, but Arnott has to do some heavy lifting to fix the problem. ■

where you want it to be.

Some of these systems are hybrids in that they start as one system but can be expanded to another. For example, Air Lift Performance offers the 3P setup, which, when upgraded with height sensors, becomes the 3H (and technically, the 3H is listed as being height and pressure). Ridetech has something similar with the RidePro X, which starts with pressure sensors and expands with height sensors.

The question here is fairly obvious: what is the advantage to one of these setups? As mentioned in the section about height-sensor-based systems, some people want a number. They need some kind of way to quantify what's going on in their setup. A pressure and height sensor system provides that. Otherwise, there's no real edge.

Installing an Air Lift Performance 3H Kit

Now you know the pros and cons of the different types of digital air management systems, so let's dive into an install.

The vehicle in question was a Chevrolet Suburban, but it wasn't going into the shop to get laid out. Instead, the owner wanted height adjustability to make entering and exiting the vehicle easier. (Photo Courtesy Switch Suspension)

To determine the truck's original ride height, a series of measurements was taken and recorded at all four corners. (Photo Courtesy Switch Suspension)

The height of the passenger's seat was also measured, as this was the main point of concern. (Photo Courtesy Switch Suspension)

Laying out all of the parts before an install makes it easier to find everything once you confirm that you have the parts you need. (Photo Courtesy Switch Suspension)

Installing the Air System Components

The plan was to put as much of the setup as possible in the front of the vehicle. To make that happen, the front bumper cover was removed, and the air tank installed behind the bumper support. (Photo Courtesy Switch Suspension)

There was room on the driver's side of the fender well, so the team at Switch Suspension built a bracket to hold the two Viair 444 compressors and the Air Lift Performance 3H manifold. (Photo Courtesy Switch Suspension)

The compressors were then covered with a plate, and the 3H manifold bolted on top. This provided plenty of room for the air line connections and kept them away from the heat of the engine. (Photo Courtesy Switch Suspension)

Installing the Airbags

The rear suspension didn't require much modification. The stock springs were removed and the axle was prepped for bag mounts to locate where the top mounts sat. Then, the new saddles were installed onto the axle. (Photo Courtesy Switch Suspension)

The rear airbag was test fitted in place. The lower mount still needed to be welded in place, but this gives you an idea of the basic placement. (Photo Courtesy Switch Suspension)

The front suspension of the Suburban is a little bit different. It has an upper and lower control arm with a strut assembly supporting the weight of the truck. It was removed and disassembled, leaving the crew with just a strut to work with. (Photo Courtesy Switch Suspension)

The strut caps needed some modification so that they wouldn't rub on the airbag. To make that work, some of the metal was removed and then smoothed out with a grinder. (Photo Courtesy Switch Suspension)

Here's the completed strut that is ready for reinstallation. (Photo Courtesy Switch Suspension)

Finally, the strut is installed into the suspension. Once the air lines are run, this bag will be able to function normally. (Photo Courtesy Switch Suspension)

Installing the 3H Height Sensors

The height sensor mounts have an arm that needs to connect to a moving suspension part. In this case, a custom bracket was made and built to hold the linkage onto the control arm. (Photo Courtesy Switch Suspension)

The completed truck does sit lower, but not so low that you couldn't drive it if the system failed for any reason. (Photo Courtesy Switch Suspension)

Final measurements show a roughly 4-inch drop overall, making life a lot easier for the passengers in this Suburban. (Photo Courtesy Switch Suspension)

A similar setup happens in the rear with one of the upper links. The idea is to measure the height between the holes in the sensor arm and the mounting point (both all the way down and all the way up). Then, follow a chart listed in the manual to determine which of the three holes on the sensor that you'll mount it to. (Photo Courtesy Switch Suspension)

SUSPENSIONS

By this point, you know all about the various components involved in an airbag setup and how they function together. However, what you haven't yet seen is the suspension of a vehicle and how everything works in harmony.

Since the fundamentals of suspensions haven't yet been covered, that is tackled next, and there's a lot to be considered. Let's start with a question that people new to airbags often ask: do you need shocks and sway bars?

Shock Absorbers

In a word: yes. In several words: absolutely, otherwise you're going to hate your vehicle. This is why: shock absorbers perform in tandem with the coil spring on the vehicle. While the coil holds up the weight of the vehicle and lets it travel up and down in the suspension, the shock dampens the ride in both directions. That dampening is critical to keeping your ride nausea-free.

Cruise down a bumpy road sometime and you'll feel the advantages of shock absorbers. Without them, you'd oscillate up and down for what seems like forever. It's a very floaty feeling, and not a lot of fun. Shocks smooth all of that out. They take the broad up-and-down movement and make it cleaner and crisper.

Some people with bagged vehicles don't run shocks. They say there's just not the room or they don't want to spend the extra money. In addition, there's also a widely disproven theory that airbags are more like shocks than coils, so you get a better ride anyway. That's just not the case. Airbags are coils with an adjustable height. Shocks are still shocks no matter what.

Why don't people want to run them? Well out back, space is usually not a problem, particularly in a truck. However, up front, depending on the vehicle, it can get a little tight in the fender well, and installing a shock can get hairy. For example, it means

This front suspension is almost ready for its airbag installation.

The shock absorber in the center of the control arm is part of a kit that Todd at Lowboy Motorsports makes for Chevrolet duallies. Without that shock, the front of the truck would float uncontrollably and make the truck extremely difficult to drive.

This once-blue shock absorber now is bare metal because the wheel and tire come in contact with it when turning. It's less than ideal, and the setup was fixed. It illustrates why some people don't want to run shocks.

that the vehicle may have a smaller turning radius, and there's the fear that the rim might rub against it.

However, the drawbacks are much greater. At the end of the day, it comes down to safety. If the truck is floating down the road and the tires are floating too, the stopping distance increases. Going without shocks means risking an accident, and that's not good for anyone.

Yes, you need shock absorbers. They may cost more than you like, and they could get in the way of your wheels. However, they're important, and you want them on your ride every time.

Sway Bars

Not every vehicle comes standard with a sway bar, and there aren't always aftermarket options. However, let's take a moment and talk about the concept as a whole.

The idea behind a sway bar is pretty simple. When a car or truck turns into a corner, its natural tendency is to lean so that the side that's on the inside of the corner raises up and the opposite end squats down. It may be fun to do that, but it's not very safe. In an ideal world, you want your tires and suspension flat through a corner at speed because it provides better traction and stability.

A sway bar helps to sort out this problem by tying the two sides of the suspension together. On a truck, such as a 1995 Chevrolet Silverado, it's bolted to the frame in the middle and then tied to the lower control arms with bushings. In some other vehicles, it connects to a mount on the struts. It just depends on what you're building.

While that 1995 Chevrolet Silverado comes standard with a sway bar, not all trucks do—not even all 1995 Chevrolet full-size pickups. A Toyota pickup of the same era did not, and those are also very popular with the mini-truck airbag community. Many compact cars do not come standard with them, either. So, do you need a sway bar?

A sway bar is not required in every vehicle. Some people like to remove them even if their ride has one from the factory, and others want to add them when they're not there. The general rule of thumb is that if it came from the dealership with a sway bar, leave it on.

With that being said, there are reasons why you may want to remove it.

Some people want to dance their airbagged vehicle in car shows. It's not quite as popular as it used to be, but it is a thing, and some love it. In that situation, a sway bar gets in the way, as it stops the car or truck from hitting those deep sides. One could argue that they should leave the actual sway bar in there, and then remove the end links when performing.

The other motivation for removing the sway bar is to fit wider wheels. Sway bars often get in the way of vehicles with tighter clearances (like the aforementioned Toyota pickup), and having one just means having another thing to rub your tires or rims against when turning. In those situations, it might be okay if it's removed.

Custom-built off-road vehicles are famous for having quick-disconnect sway-bar end links. That way, they can get the most articulation when climbing. It's not something that most custom car and truck people do, but it's certainly an option.

A sway bar is a solid improvement for your vehicle, particularly if it's bagged. Not only will it handle better overall but the argument could also be made that it's safer too.

Independent Suspensions

There are many various types of independent suspensions out there. They can be found on both front- and rear-wheel-drive vehicles, and each one requires a different type of installation.

So, let's talk about the first thing, which is the difference between independent and dependent suspensions. In simplest terms, look at a truck. Most trucks today have an independent front suspension, where each corner can lift and lower separately from another (whether or not there's a sway bar). On the back of the truck is a straight axle, and that's a dependent suspension. When one corner goes up, the opposite one goes down, and there's no getting around that movement. It can be minimized but never removed entirely.

There are many different types of independent suspensions. What follows is by no mean an exhaustive list, but it covers a lot of the kinds that you'll run into on a regular basis.

Struts and Double Wishbone Suspensions

The idea with these setups is that you have an upper and lower control arm connected with a steering knuckle. They can move up and down independently and are designed for both front- and rear-wheel-drive vehicles.

The ride is handled by a strut. This is a shock absorber that has a coil placed around it with a cap on the top. You can remove a strut and coil as an entire assembly, which makes it pretty easy to pull in and out of a vehicle. If you buy strut airbags, you can bolt those right in too.

Another aspect to note is that a strut in this type of configuration does not turn, which provides flexibility in how you set up the suspension for airbags.

This is the front suspension on a 2005 Chrysler 300C, which is a popular car to bag. In these scenarios, you need to get some kind of strut bag. Universal Air Suspension sells a strut bag kit for these cars starting at $920.

MacPherson Strut Suspensions

A MacPherson strut is very similar to a traditional strut suspension, in that the spring and shock assembly can be removed as one unit. However, a MacPherson strut itself is quite different.

Both setups have a lower control arm and a steering knuckle. There is no upper control arm in a MacPherson-strut suspension, however. Instead, the strut bolts to the knuckle directly, and then the top of the strut turns with the wheel.

Bagging these cars is a little bit more difficult but certainly not impossible. Companies such as Universal Air Suspension have kits for MacPherson-strut cars, as do others, so there are options. However, one thing to consider is how you route the air lines. Since they're in the fender well and your wheels will turn, make sure the lines are properly secured and won't rub at any point in the strut's arc.

Coil Spring Suspensions

Onward to the ubiquitous coil spring setups. These have two unequal-length control arms connected by a steering knuckle at one end with a spring in the frame or a pocket. You'll find these in most Chevy trucks and cars from the 1960s on up, and they're quite popular to use for airbags.

Depending on the year, make, and model of your vehicle, there may be trimming required to make the airbag fit.

Twist Beam or Torsion Bar Suspensions

The concept of a torsion bar is pretty cool. Basically, it's a piece of spring steel that's a straight rod with splines on both ends. When it's installed, one end is put inside a keyed end at the base of a lower control arm, while the other keyed end goes into a torsion bar key that's bolted to the frame. As the vehicle (most often a truck) goes up and down, the torsion bar twists. One end turns with the control arm, and the other is locked in place. It's essentially a replacement for a spring, and it's great for both four-wheel-drive trucks and mini trucks where there's not a lot of room for a coil.

Of course, trucks with torsion bars get bagged regularly, so how does that work?

Sometimes people keep their torsion bars and add an airbag. On the plus side, it means they have two things supporting the weight of the truck: the torsion bar and the air-

bag. On the downside, it means they *only* have two things supporting the weight of the truck, and they can work against each other. On top of that, it likely won't be as low.

So, the more-common option is to remove the torsion bars entirely and replace them with airbags. There's no downside here assuming that the bags are installed properly.

Bolt-In Crossmembers

While some cars and trucks need cutting and fabrication to lay down, others can be all bolt-on. In some older muscle cars as well as the 1960–1987 Chevy C-10 pickups, the front crossmember can be unbolted and replaced with a new one. Those new crossmembers are designed to be completely modern replacements, which means big brakes, better handling, rack-and-pinion steering, and, in some cases, bag mounts.

This coil spring suspension is on a 2004 Chevrolet Silverado, and it's the same basic setup as there's been on Chevy trucks since 1960.

The chassis of this 1972 Chevrolet Blazer frame features an aftermarket bolt-in front crossmember. These types of systems have integrated bag mounts as well as setups for the engine and steering.

The CBC Pro kit on this 1973 Chevrolet Silverado is a complete front cross-member with the rack and pinion, engine mounts, bag mounts, and suspension components integrated. See how that bag mount is positioned so that it pairs with the lower control arms? That's an important feature that you get with this kind of kit. (Photo Courtesy Switch Suspension)

The downside? They're not cheap. If you have, say, a 1973–1987 Chevrolet truck, a front crossmember from CBC Pro will run you somewhere north of $2,500, depending on the options and supplier you choose. It's worth every penny for a number of reasons, including ease of installation. However, you have to weigh the decision based on your budget.

As a broad statement, if a bolt-in crossmember is available for your vehicle and it will not only make the airbag installation easier but also modernize your suspension, then go for it. If it's only one of those things or neither, consider going another route.

Straight-Axle Suspensions

In the back of most trucks and some rear-wheel drive cars sits an axle. Usually, that axle is held to the chassis via leaf springs, but sometimes it's held with trailing arms and coils or something similar. Either way, it's not only important how the power from the engine gets to the ground but also where you need to start to bag your ride.

But before this all ramps up, there is an important prequalification: this is not an extensive deep dive into the world of instant center, pinion angles, bell crank suspensions, and the like. There are literally entire books about those topics, and as such, it's best to pick up one of those if you're interested.

Instead, the following content provides a basic overview of some types of suspensions that you can use to put airbags on a straight-axle vehicle, including the pros and cons. You may personally disagree with some of the calls made here, and that's your prerogative. The point is that this will get you started.

There are a few items to discuss because the rear end is different from the front. It's at this point that geometry comes into play.

First, let's discuss the axle itself. If the vehicle has leaf springs (and lots of trucks do), they're serving two purposes: supporting the vehicle and keeping the axle located in relation to the frame. Leaf springs are great, but when it comes time to lower a vehicle, they're limiting. You need to find a different way to keep the axle centered and aligned through its range of travel. There are many different ways to do this, but for airbagged vehicles (for the most part), consider either a two-link, three-link, four-link, and/or a Watts link.

Whatever suspension you choose, it must do three things. The first is to keep the axle laterally located in the chassis, whether it's through the link system or the addition of a Panhard bar or Watts link. Second, it needs to give the axle a path to travel up and down in the chassis to allow for movement as the vehicle is driven down the street. Third, an axle is heavy. The link system must keep it from rolling forward or aft. This means that you can't just put a link with an eyelet on the bottom of an axle because without something up top, it will roll over.

Let's go over the options.

Two-Link Suspensions

The simplest kind of rear suspension for a truck is called a two-link. It involves two parallel bars that run along the side of the frame and mount at a pivot point. They're then bolted to the underside of the axle just like a traditional leaf spring. This allows the axle to move up and down in an arc.

The advantage here comes in with how the bars are set up. If they're super long, you can put a bag mount at a point that's closer to the pivot than usual, giving you a 2:1 or even 3:1 ratio. That means if you want to lift the rear of your truck with a bag that gets 8 inches of lift, you end up with 24 inches of total height if you do a 3:1 ratio. That's a lot of lift. Plus, since the bag has more strain on it and is carrying a heavier load from a leverage perspective, the ride can be very soft. You also don't need a Panhard bar or anything else to locate the axle laterally in the chassis, which saves space.

So that's the perfect option, right? Well, no. One problem with a two-link is the lack of pivots. Since the axle is bolted directly to the bar, the pinion angle (the relationship between the pinion on the axle and the driveshaft) is going to go through sweeping changes, which is never good for the longevity of your axle, driveshaft, or transmission. There's also no articulation; when one side of the car or truck lifts, so does the other. So, a soft suspension may not actually handle very well. There can also be some wheel hop out of it too, or you may find the back end lifting when you brake or take off.

There are many people who use two-link suspensions, and they work. However, it's up to you to decide if you like that idea or not and whether you want to use it in your build.

Three-Link Suspensions

This type of link setup has many variations but the same basic theme. Like the two-link, there are two trailing arms set up from the frame to the bottom of the axle. But now, the mounts on the axles have a pivot point, which means that the top of the axle also needs some kind of support. The solution is handled in one of a few different ways.

The first is found in drag cars mostly, although some off-road vehicles use this method too. There's a single link bar placed parallel with the bottom bars that's mounted on top of the pumpkin. That bar is approximately 70 percent of the length of the bottom trailing-arm bar.

The second option is another

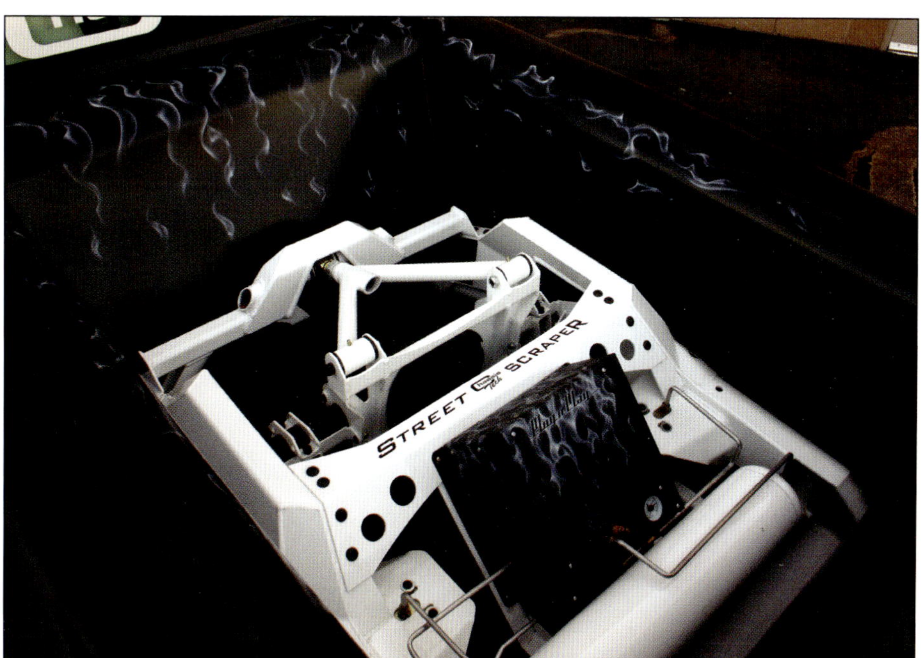

This is a variation on the triangulated three-link suspension. Note that there are two pivots on the axle but they meet at one point on a new custom crossmember.

Bag Ratios and Strength

In a two- or three-link setup, the airbag is typically positioned somewhere on one of the lower links. This way, more lift and a potentially softer ride can be achieved. However, if you do that, be sure to properly reinforce the link arm. Otherwise, you will bend it.

When put in a position where the airbag is using leverage, there's more pressure put on all of its connections. If the link bar is small, not gusseted, or just made of thinner materials, it won't be able to handle the extra weight placed on it. As a result, it will fail and potentially cause an accident.

For this reason, many two-link builders fabricate their links out of leaf-spring bushings and square tubing. That gives them a way to bolt the arms into the stock leaf-spring locations, and the square tubing (if it's thick enough) is beefy enough to handle the extra load.

What you can't do is take a simple bolt-on or weld-on four-link kit, slap a bag mount on it, and call it good. That's a guaranteed way to see the links bend and get into an accident. ■

Visualizing Pinion Angle

There are many things to consider with various link styles, but one to think about is the pinion angle. As already noted, the more the pinion angle changes, the more havoc can be played on the transmission, bearings, etc. Fortunately, there's a way to see it in action. Make yourself a cardboard mock-up of the links and axle, and using pins, guide the suspension up and down the range of travel. Otherwise, you can just watch a video of someone who did exactly that. Search for "Suspension Link Video" by Joel Liss for a good visual representation of this concept. ■

bar that goes around the approximate area of one of the trailing-arm mounting points and comes in diagonally toward the differential. This also serves the purpose of stopping the top of the axle from rolling.

Finally, some people take the concept of a triangulated four-link and tweak it to form a wishbone three-link. In that case, there are two bars located on the top of the axle tubes. These triangulate into one pivot point on a mount made in the middle of the chassis.

All three of these options typically also run a Panhard bar, although the wishbone three-link does not always follow that rule out in the wild.

So, first off, there are many links going on here, particularly with the Panhard. However, if you're looking to keep the gas tank in the stock location (a common reason to want a two- or three-link suspension) or you just don't have the space to do something with a triangulated upper link setup, this could work for you. The downside is that if you do anything on top of the pumpkin, there's going to be a lot of cutting for clearance in the trunk or bed. There's a lot of math involved in this one to make sure everything is set up properly.

Four-Link Suspensions

A four-link can be done in one of two ways, but they serve the same purpose: allow the axle to travel up and down while keeping it centered side to side in the frame.

The first option is a triangulated four-link. Like the other setups, this has two trailing arms going from the frame to the bottom of the axle, and both points pivot. Up top, two more link bars with pivots are in place, and they run from the sides of the chassis toward the middle of the axle (some variations reverse this setup as well so that the tip of the triangle is on a mount in the lateral center of the chassis). These setups do not need a Panhard bar or any other kind of lateral axle location, as the triangulated bars do that job.

The second choice is a parallel four-link. Again, two trailing arms with pivots on both ends run from the chassis to the axle. However, now there's a second set of bars just above

Here's another take on a three-link, and like the one shown prior, it's triangulated. However, this time, there's just one pivot on the axle, and it's centered.

This is a parallel four-link shown during installation, so it doesn't yet have a Panhard bar. However, it still serves a purpose: it allows the axle to move up and down with the airbags.

Bag Location

Now that you know about all of the various types of link systems for cars or trucks with a rear axle, where do you place the bag in those scenarios? There are many ways to do it, so what works best if you're using a traditional double-convoluted airbag?

One common option is called "bag over axle," and it is just that: a bracket is welded to the top of the axle and the frame, and the bag is placed between the two. This is arguably the easiest option because everything is very straightforward. However, it (like everything else) has advantages and disadvantages.

On the plus side, it has the best towing capacity because the bag is in a 1:1 ratio. So, if you bag your dually and want to tow a fifth wheel, this is your jam. The downside? Well, it doesn't usually ride very well, particularly at higher pressures. If you are rocking a dually though, you might not notice thanks to the extra weight. Also, these types of setups take up the most room, as you have the height of the compressed bag to deal with, plus the additional height of the frame to support the upper notch.

If you mount the bag in the back of the axle, you'll get slightly less lift than you would with it on top. The opposite is true if the bag is in front of the axle (you'll get more lift). The thing is that it's a negligible difference either way, and in both cases, you gain a little bit more floor room. This is why older bagged cars often put the bag in one of these two spots, as it saves space in the trunk and back seat location. ■

---

the first that mounts on top of the axle. These arms are parallel with each other per side, and per pair. They also need some kind of lateral axle-locating device, such as a Panhard bar.

Four-links (both parallel and tri-angulated) take up a lot of space, and on a mini truck or small car, that can be at a premium. However, these setups ride quite nicely and handle well too. As a result, they're fairly popular.

Panhard Bars and Other Lateral Axle Locators

Did you notice a common thread among all those types of links? Most of them need some kind of lateral locator for the axle. But why?

Whatever kind of link setup you choose, they're mainly designed to control the vertical motion of the axle. If you're looking at the truck from the side, it's how the axle is controlled up and down in the chassis. However, if you were to try to push an axle side to side that doesn't have a lateral locator, it would shift, and

Here's a Panhard bar on a 2000 Chevrolet Silverado. It's located on the bottom of the axle on the passenger's side and then runs up to a mount on the driver's side of the frame. This is how the axle stays centered laterally in the chassis.

that's bad for not only the driveline and transmission but also your physical health as well. It's just not safe.

The solution is a way to keep the axle centered side to side, and the most common one is a Panhard bar. You can find these stock on some 1967–1972 Chevrolet C-10 trucks as well as other cars of the era. The idea is that there's a bar with a pivot point that mounts to the frame and the other end of the bar (also with

a pivot) is mounted to the axle. It's pretty straightforward.

The catch is that those stock vehicles weren't made for wide ranges of movement like you'll get with airbags. When you're talking about going from 0 to 12 inches or more, that's a lot to ask from a Panhard bar. You need to really dial it in to ensure that it works correctly.

Why? Here's a little experiment. Take a piece of paper, two pencils,

---

and a bit of string. Now, tie the two pencils together, making sure that the distance between them is pretty short (maybe 3-4 inches). Place one pencil in your left hand and keep it still. This is going to be your originating pivot point. Now, take the other pencil, pull it tight against the first, and draw an arc. That arc is the travel if the string is your Panhard bar. It's a way to visualize that the more the axle travels up and down in the chassis, the more the Panhard bar pulls the axle side to side, potentially causing your tires to hit the sides of the body.

So, that means a few things. First, set up the Panhard bar so that it's parallel to the ground when you're at the middle of the suspension's travel. That way, the axle won't shift too far to the left or the right when you raise or lower the vehicle. Second, the longer the Panhard bar, the less arc you'll have overall. Try to push it so that the bar goes all the way to the opposite side of the axle, and you'll be fine.

Of course, there is a method that ensures the axle won't move dramatically from side to side, and that is a Watts link.

This is a Watts link kit sold by KP Components (part of Chris Alston's Chassisworks) to complement its bolt-on cantilever kit, but it works with all sorts of other link setups too.

Watts Links

With a Panhard bar, there is one piece of tubing that controls the lateral direction of the axle. With a Watts link, there are two pieces of tubing and a pivot.

The idea is that there's a mount on the center of the axle, and that mount holds a vertical section that has a pivot of its own in the middle. The two pieces of tubing (each with their own pivots) bolt to the top and bottom of that vertical section and then to the frame on their respective sides.

This sounds complicated, and, well, it is. In addition, it's not perfect. If you have a vehicle with a narrow frame, it can be difficult to figure out where to mount everything. It's also complicated logistically to figure out if you're building one on your own, and they can limit travel if the arms aren't long enough.

But it has its advantages. A properly set up Watts link keeps the axle centered side to side no matter where it is in the arc. That's pretty impressive, particularly when dealing with a vehicle that can see a lot of travel. However, it's a lot more complex than a Panhard bar and doesn't work for every situation. Consider both heavily before you dive in too deep.

Installing a Watts Link

So, you have the basic idea of how a Watts link works. This the installation.

Prepping for Installation

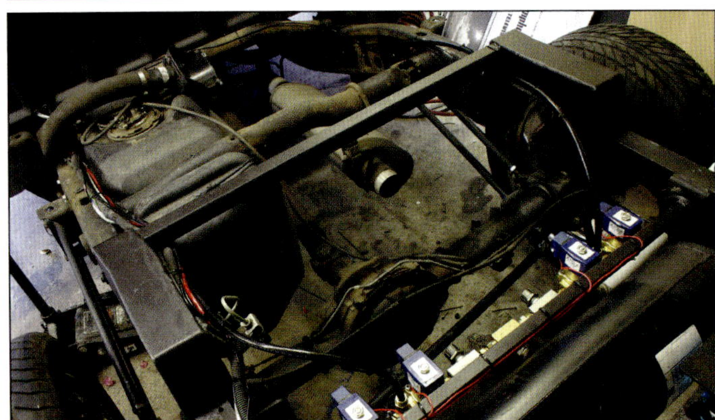

1 *This truck started with a Panhard bar but needed an upgrade.*

2 *The center link needs to be assembled first off the truck. That starts with lubricating the bushings and installing them in the linkage.*

3 *The center link is then bolted into the center section. The recommended torque requirements are in the instructions.*

4 *The mount bolts to the existing differential. To get it on, unbolt the stock cover (leaving it in place, as we're not replacing it) and then install the Watts-link mount over it. Then, bolt it all together using the supplied longer hardware and lock washers.*

Installing the Linkage

1 *Each end of the Watts-link arms use Heim joints. When you first bolt everything up, install them halfway in on both sides. Also, make sure to keep both links the same length.*

2 *The links are bolted to the center link on the axle. At this point, everything is kept fairly loose to make sure the installation goes smoothly, but it will all be torqued down once it's done.*

3 *With the links bolted to the brackets, they're located on the frame. Then, the mounting holes are marked for drilling. The same process happens on the other side.*

4 *Now, the mounting holes are drilled using progressively larger bits.*

5 *Using the provided backing plate, the brackets are bolted to the frame using a ratcheting wrench and a socket wrench.*

6 *The completed setup is now ready to go. As the suspension travels up and down, the center link adjusts in a "smooth S" pattern, keeping the axle centered in the chassis.*

INSTALLATIONS

By now, you have a handle on the way airbags work: how they get air, lift, support a vehicle, provide ride, and are managed. However, it's time to see all of this in real-world scenarios where you can see some of the ways that airbags work and the types of things to avoid.

This is not an all-encompassing list by any means. People install airbags on truck beds, golf carts, and even shopping carts, so there's a lot of variety out there. The idea is to include some of the more popular applications into this book. That way, you'll have an idea of what you're working with.

Frame and Body Modifications

The thing about fitting your airbags is that you need to be sure that they don't rub on anything. Should your airbag rub against something, it will eventually fail, leaving you stranded somewhere. Obviously, that's not a good look, so that has to be sorted out.

Sometimes you get lucky and you don't have to make any frame or body modifications to fit an airbag. In other cases, you need to do a lot of cutting to make it work. It just depends on the vehicle.

With that in mind, let's walk through the installation of airbags on a 1995 Chevrolet Silverado. These trucks require some cutting up front to make them work. Out back, the frame needs to be notched. All in all, there's a lot of frame work on these trucks, but the result is well worth it.

Disassembling the Front Suspension

1 With the truck on jack stands and the wheels removed, the first big step is taking off the brakes. To do so, the calipers are unbolted and hung from the frame, the cotter pin is removed from the spindle, and the spindle castle nut is unbolted. Once the rotor is pulled off, you're left with what is shown.

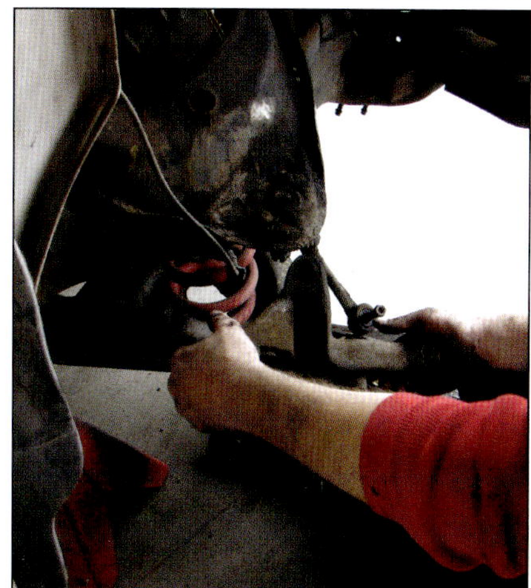

2 With a jack underneath the lower control arm, the spindle is removed from the upper and lower arms by removing the cotter pins and unbolting the ball joints. Once the jack is lowered, the spring will be mostly free from pressure. The shock has to come out before it can be removed completely.

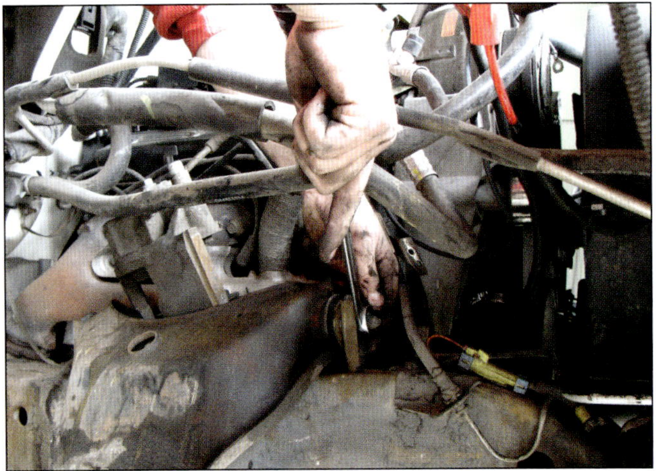

3 *This particular airbag kit comes with new upper and lower control arms that help correct the camber and provide a mounting point for the airbag and shock. As such, the upper control arm has to come off at this point.*

4 *Once the shock is unbolted and removed from the frame and lower control arm, the jack is lowered, and the spring is taken out. Now, the lower control arm is ready to be removed.*

Cutting the Frame for Airbag Clearance

1 *To begin, a rough starting point is mapped out on the frame. This is about where the bag will sit, and although it may seem like a lot, it'll get reinforced before all is said and done.*

2 *The easiest way to cut out the frame is using a plasma cutter. It'll require some cleanup later, but it's fast and efficient. If you don't have one, a reciprocating saw and cut-off wheel can do the job too.*

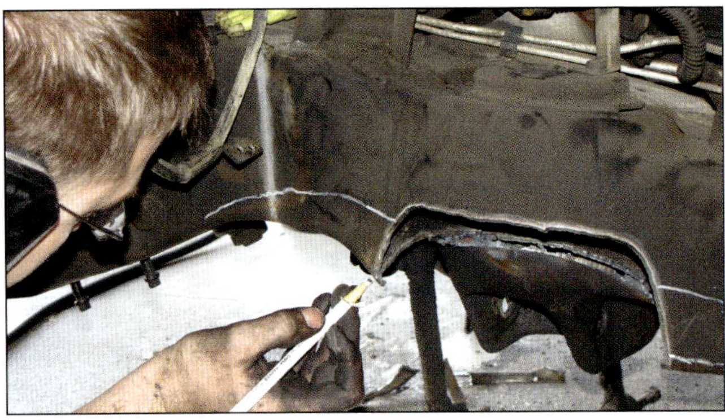

3 *There are two other areas to clearance on the frame, and these are done for two reasons. First, the tie-rod ends will hit the frame, so they need more room. Second, the lower control arm will contact the frame too. This truck was designed to lay frame on 22-inch wheels, but if you went with bigger wheels, you might have to do more cutting.*

4 *Once everything is removed with a plasma cutter, this is what's left. Again, it may look scary, but it'll all get reinforced along the way.*

5 *Using a hammer, the bottom of the frame is banged up into place to close up the pie cuts. See how the new lower control arm is mounted? It's to verify that it has enough clearance throughout its travel.*

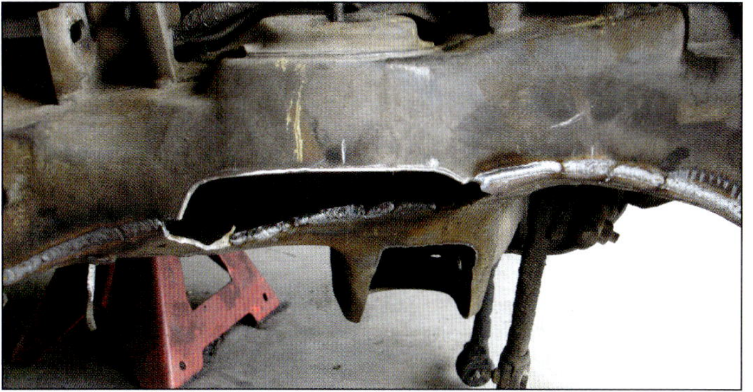

6 *The frame is now welded up solid. You could leave it just like this, but grinding it down takes it to another level.*

7 *With all the welds ground smooth, it's time to test fit the bags.*

Putting Together the Airbag/Cup Assembly

1 *To maximize the lift, you need the airbag to be fully deflated once the truck hits the ground. You also need some space between the top of the frame and the airbag. To do both, you have to install a cup like this one, which is designed to bolt into the mounting points on top of the airbag.*

2 *You may have to do some test fitting to make sure it's the right height, but it's easy enough to cut down a cup if necessary. That's exactly what happened here, and the new, shorter cup is the one that was ultimately installed.*

Test Fitting the Airbags

1 *Everything is bolted back up and test fitted together. Clearances are checked to ensure that the bag won't rub, and the amount of drop is verified.*

2 *Since this truck will run a 22-inch wheel with a 265/35ZR22 tire, a set was bolted on and the truck was set down on its own weight. This way, firewall clearance can be easily checked.*

3 *It fits, but barely. The plan with this truck was also to do a stock-floor body drop later on, so cutting out the firewall was a must.*

Clearancing the Firewall for the Wheels

1 *On the driver's side, the engine harness was in the way, so it had to be moved.*

2 *The fix here was pretty simple. First, the stock harness hole on the firewall was cut out.*

3 *Now, that piece was used to make a template on some fresh sheet metal of the same thickness.*

4 *The stock harness mount was then relocated underneath the brake booster and rotated slightly. This not only gave the tires the room they needed but also didn't require extending any of the wiring.*

5 *Using a tape measure, the cuts on the firewall are laid out with a permanent marker. The idea here is to go the distance needed for the truck to lay the body on the ground (2.75 inches) and still have at least a half inch of room for the wheels.*

6 *Using part of a trailer fender as a template, this is the resulting mark.*

Tubbing the Inner Fenders for Clearance

1 *A similar process happens for the inner fenders. The easiest way to do this is to place the fender alongside the wheel area and measure how much extra room is needed. Once that's done, a trailer fender can be tack welded in place.*

2 *Now, the inner fender can be cut out, which is done with a cut-off wheel on an angle grinder. This has to be done carefully around the fender lip, as it's quite close to the outer fender skin. Unless you want to repaint the fender, be careful at this point as well.*

3 *With the inner fender out, any smaller pieces that are left can be tack welded to the trailer fender.*

4 *It's pretty difficult to smooth out these welds because of how close they are to the upper lip. So instead, seam sealer is put over them and smoothed out with a wet finger. The result is a clean edge.*

Front Shock Installation on a 1995 Chevrolet Silverado

Now it's time to watch get the shocks get mounted. There are many different ways to do this depending on the kind of suspension you have and your goals for the vehicle.

This particular setup is pretty universal. The Chevrolet front suspension has been in use for decades on cars and trucks, and it has been copied for use with other manufacturers as well. Having a shock outside of the control arms is also quite common, even in stock vehicles. So, while you may not have a 1995 Chevrolet Silverado, it's closer to a 1960 C-10 or a newer Dodge Ram than you might think.

Installing the Upper Shock Mount

1 *These shock absorber mounts were made for the 1988–1998 Chevrolet Silverado, but they're fairly universal in design. Essentially, all you need is an upper mount for the shock; the bottom will go to the lower control arm, which, in this case, has a lower shock mount built in.*

2 *After cutting a radius in the left shock mount to clearance for the airbag, it's held in place, and the mounting holes are marked. The idea is to set it where it's in line with the lower control arm mount. That way, it doesn't bind through travel. If necessary, you can bolt the shock in there temporarily just to ballpark the placement.*

3 *The mounting holes are then drilled into the frame with the required-size bit. The hole only has to be through one side of the frame, as you can access the inside through the spring pocket.*

4 *Now, the mount is bolted into place. Again, the nuts are installed by putting an arm and wrench into the frame and tightening it down from the outside.*

Cantilever Suspensions

It's time to talk about the airbag and where it fits into the whole equation. There are a few basic scenarios here, and again, it all comes down to math.

If you mount the airbags on top of the axle and build an upper mount across the frame, the airbag will lift at a 1:1 ratio. This means that if your airbag has 8 inches of lift, the rear of the truck will get 8 inches of travel overall from fully deflated to completely inflated.

That's a perfectly acceptable option, and many people choose to do it because, in that scenario, the airbag is working exactly as intended. If you plan on doing some towing or something similar, the airbags will

These airbags are mounted on top of the axle, which is commonly referred to as "bag over axle." It'll give the back end a 1:1 lift ratio, so if the airbag gets 6 inches of lift, the rear end will also lift 6 inches.

support their rated load, and everything will be perfect. The ride quality will fluctuate depending on how much pressure is in the bag. Otherwise, you're good to go.

What if you want a little bit more lift and you're willing to give up some of your capacity? What if you'd like a little bit softer ride? Well in those scenarios, you have to move the bag to a different location—one that will provide a better ratio. That's

where cantilever installations come into play.

There are many ways to do a cantilever suspension, and they all involve basic math. For the sake of this discussion, let's say that the vehicle in question has a triangulated four-link and the bottom two arms are going to be used for the cantilever. If you placed the airbag halfway between the pivot on the frame and the pivot on the axle, you would be

lifting at a 2:1 ratio. If you moved it even farther toward the pivot on the axle, the ratio would go even higher (to maybe 2.5 or 3:1) depending on the length of the bar.

Now, there are things to watch out for here. The bar you're using for the bag mount must be beefed up to support the load. A heavy gusset on the bottom and/or thicker construction is also necessary. Otherwise, you'll bend the bars or cause them to flex when you drive. Also, know that the farther down the bar you go, the softer the ride will be and the less capacity you'll have. If you plan on doing anything strenuous with the vehicle, that's definitely something to consider.

Overall, cantilever kits are very popular—so much so that many manufacturers make setups that incorporate some kind of cantilever design.

Installing a Cantilever Suspension Kit

KP Components, which is part of Chris Alston's Chassisworks, has been making cantilever kits for years now. These bolt-on designs replace the factory leaf springs entirely and replace them with a parallel four-link, Panhard bar, or Watts link and a cantilever bracket system. It's great for full-size trucks and rides well too.

Taking Apart the Rear Suspension

1 *Starting the rear cantilever kit installation process means first removing all the stock stuff. With that in mind, the leaf springs are unbolted and set in the recycling pile.*

2 The kit requires that you remove the stock leaf spring mounts from the frame, and that's not fun to do. The easiest way is to cut an "X" shape in the head of the rivet using a cut-off wheel. Then, use an air chisel to punch the remaining rivet out of the frame.

3 Once the heads are gone, a chisel and hammer will knock the bracket off the frame. An air chisel comes in handy here too, as it helps make removing the old rivet easier.

4 Normally, this kit bolts onto the axle. However, because the previous owner installed a leaf-spring flip kit, those brackets need to come off. For that, a plasma cutter is the easiest tool, but a cut-off wheel will do in a pinch. Once the tabs are off, the axle tube is ground down smooth with a grinder.

Mounting the Brackets

1 The kit comes with axle brackets that incorporate mounts for the parallel four-link, the cantilever links, and the Panhard bar. They're attached using the included U-bolts and hardware.

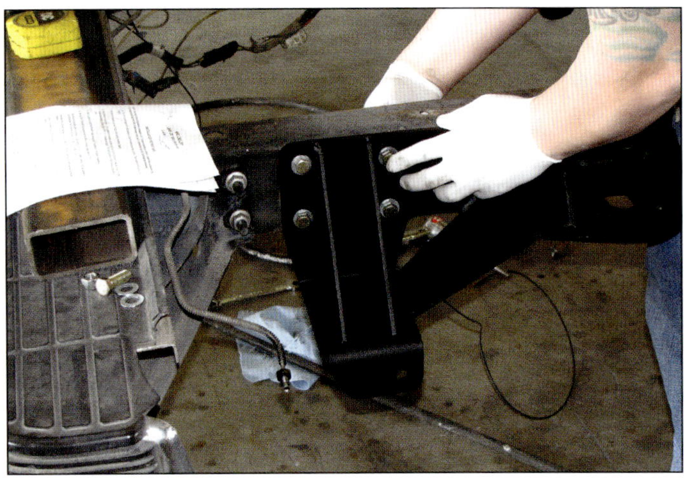

2 Now, it's time to bolt the rear cantilever brackets in place. A few of the holes are already in the frame, but additional ones need to be drilled out as well. Fortunately, you can use the brackets as a guide and a punch to mark the holes, making the process go a little smoother.

3 The front brackets go on in the same fashion. These hold the parallel four-link bars in place.

Installing the Linkage

1 All of the bushings on the links are assembled using the included grease and sleeves. It's not always easy to press everything together by hand. A bench vise comes in handy in this situation.

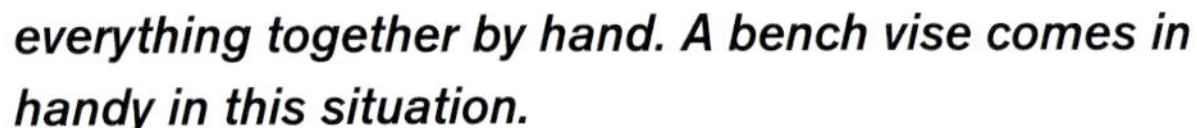

2 The cantilever link arms go on next. The dog bone between the arm with the bag plate and the axle allows the cantilever to work in harmony with the parallel four-link so that they don't pull against each other. Also, notice that the link bar is reinforced at the bottom with a gusset to provide extra strength.

3 The final links to mount are the parallel four-link and the Panhard bar. They bolt to the brackets and complete the basic setup.

Frame Modifications and Other Tips

If you're looking to build a vehicle that's low, one possible option is to notch the frame. Why? Because the axle will only travel so far before it hits the chassis, and if your goal is to put it on the ground and you're not there yet, then a notch is the only way to go. Well, unless it's a bridge.

A notch, or C-notch, is when a section of the frame is cut out to allow the axle to travel up higher than stock and then the hole is reinforced so that the frame doesn't buckle. This is typically done on vehicles with a static drop because you don't want to go too deep into the frame. You just want a touch more travel than you'd get from stock.

A bridge, or step notch, is when you take that to the next level. You're actually creating a steel structure that replaces the frame, and looks like, well, a bridge. With a bridge notch, you can go as high as you need to, and that includes extra room if you're doing a setup with the bags on top of the axle. This process is sometimes called "bridging" the frame.

How do you figure out how tall of a bridge you need? Math.

Let's play this into a few different scenarios. First, you have the wheels and tires that you want to run, and you just need to figure out where the bottom of the bridge needs to sit.

If you're running an 8-piece notch (like is shown in this book), it's pretty straightforward. Park the vehicle on a level surface. Measure from the lowest point of the frame to the ground. Let's call that variable "X." Then, measure from the top of the axle "X" inches. Add the thickness of the bottom of the 8-piece notch to

This is a C-notch. Although it's not technically in a "C" shape, the idea is to allow the truck's axle to travel into the frame just a little bit more than stock while still keeping the structural integrity. It does so by sandwiching two sections of 1/4-inch plate together around the stock frame, which makes everything nice and strong.

that number (variable "B"), and you have where the bottom of the sides of the notch need to sit.

Similar math works if you're building your own notch out of square tubing. Just don't worry about the thickness of the bottom of the notch because it's not an issue anymore.

The only other aspect to consider is to have a half inch to an inch or so of wiggle room. Some parts settle and air pressure in the tires may change. Giving yourself some leeway there helps. You can also accommodate a threaded bump stop, which would also have to come out of the calculations.

In the second scenario, you know what size of wheels and tires you want, but you don't have them yet. This is when the math gets more

complex. You need to know a few things:

- The distance from the ground to the lowest part of the frame, which is usually under the cab is "X"
- The overall tire height is "Y"
- The diameter of the axle is "Z"

We're also going to add in some space for buffer:

- 1 inch for wiggle room
- "B" inches for the steel on the 8-piece notch
- If you want to add an adjustable bump stop to the equation, measure its height when it's halfway installed, and then enter that after the thickness of the frame

This is the equation to use:

$$X + (Y/2) + (Z/2) + 1 + B$$

Let's say that with the truck or car on jack stands, you have 14 inches for X, you're running a 27-inch-tall tire, and your axle is 3 inches in diameter. Here's how that looks:

$$14 + (27/2) + (3/2) + 1 + 0.25 = 30.25$$

Therefore, the bottom of your step notch (before the bottom piece of the eight-piece notch is welded in) needs to be 30.25 inches from the ground.

There's a third way to do this, and this particular method works best if you're using an eight-piece notch as shown in this book.

Let's use all of the same variables as before, but this time, we need to add one more.

- The distance from the ground to the lowest part of the frame, which is usually under the cab is "X"
- The overall tire height is "Y"
- The diameter of the axle is "Z"
- The distance from the bottom of the frame where the axle will hit to the ground is "A"

Variable "A" is going to be bigger than "X." So, let's start by subtracting A from X. Then, do the same math on the tire height, axle diameter, and that extra buffer space. The equation looks like this:

$$(Y/2) + (Z/2) - (A-X) + 1$$

If we run that math through using all the same numbers as before but now with "A" in mind, we get this:

$$(27/2) + (3/2) - (24-14) + 1 = 6$$

That means if you measure from the bottom of the existing frame to the bottom of the eight-piece notch, you need there to be 6 inches. Basically, you need a 6-inch notch.

Prepping for the Bridge

1 *There are many different ways to bridge a truck, but in this case, an eight-piece notch kit is used. To start, it's lined up on the frame above the axle, and a permanent marker is used to mark where it'll be welded.*

2 *The paint on the frame is ground down with a sanding disc on a right-angle grinder. This provides a clean surface to weld to and ensures the weld is strong.*

Welding the Bridge

1 *The inner piece of the notch is welded in first. A bead is laid on the inside of the notch (both top and bottom) to ensure that it's solid.*

2 *Since this truck had a C-notch and that C-notch was welded in place, it was difficult to remove prior to installing the bridge notch. Fortunately, a cut-off wheel on a grinder made the work go a little smoother.*

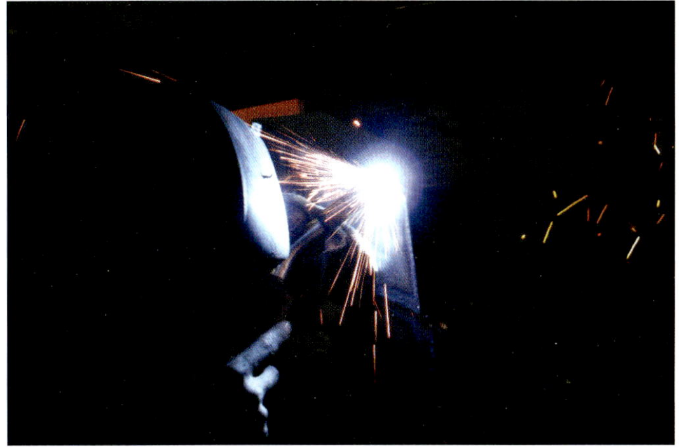

3 *Once the two sides were in place, it was time to weld the top cap. This encloses the notch, and once it's on, you can cut out the stock frame between the legs.*

4 *The finishing touch is the inside edge of the notch. It's clamped into place and then welded. Now, the frame is rock solid, and the axle can travel up a few more inches.*

Notching for the Driveline

Once you notched the frame for the axle, it's possible that the driveline on the vehicle may hit something on its way up. What's the fix? Notch the offending crossmember or sheet metal.

1 *Here's where the driveline hits: a gas tank crossmember just behind the cab. It also hits at the bottom edge of the cab, but that's fixed by hammering the lip slightly to get it out of the way.*

2 First, a piece of pipe is picked up that's wider than the diameter of the driveline. Then, it's cut in half and used as a template to mark the crossmember. A plasma cutter makes quick work of the job.

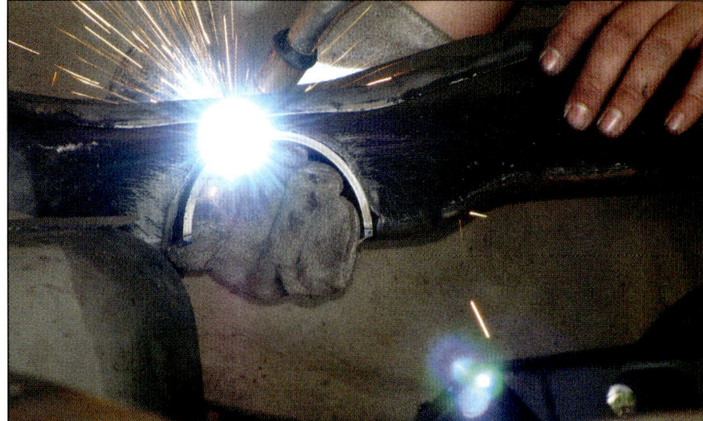

3 Then, the tubing is welded into the crossmember. Now the driveline can travel up into it with no problems or rubbing.

Making Compressor and Tank Brackets

You will need to mount a lot of items in the vehicle: tanks, valves, compressors, relays, and more. In a truck, one of the best spots is typically behind the axle. In this case, two tanks and two compressors were going back there, so some brackets needed to be made.

1 The first step is to install a rear crossmember. In this case, the idea was to put something beefy back there as not only a mounting point for other parts but also so it could be tapped for bolts instead of self-tapping screws. It's cut and then welded in place.

2 Two compressor mounts were welded to the new crossmember. First, they were tacked in place. Then, once it was confirmed that there were no clearance issues with the compressors, they were welded fully.

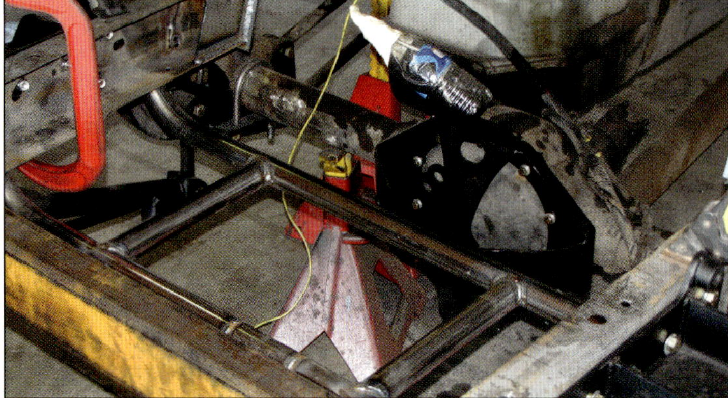

3 Using some steel tubing, a pair of tank brackets were fabricated and welded to the underside of the frame. This keeps them under the bed floor. Plus, they look cool.

4 *Once everything was done, it was all painted up in matte black to match the rest of the frame.*

Relocating Things in the Engine Bay

If your car or truck is low enough, the tires will go into the engine bay. When that happens, things that were mounted on the fenders have to be relocated. Get creative to figure out how to do so, but here are a few examples to help you along your way.

In this truck, a 1995 Chevrolet Silverado, the master cylinder and core support were used as mounting spots for a new bracket.

This bracket holds the ABS system and a fuse block so it's all out of the way of the tire, even when turning.

The fuse block and battery were both quite close to the tire under the hood of this 2004 Silverado. Thanks to a bracket for the fuse block and a few minor tweaks to the battery tray, everything worked out well.

There are other things that might get in the way that you'd never consider, such as hood springs. The ones on this truck were in the way, so they were unbolted. A Snap-on hood prop was used from that point forward, but you could also look into using shocks (such as the ones on a car's trunk) instead.

The coolant expansion tank was also mounted above the tire. The stock fender mounting point was cut out of the fender and then welded to a new spot closer to the core support and out of the way of the tire.

Front-Wheel Drive Suspensions

Most rear-wheel-drive vehicles have a pretty similar bag setup. The axle usually has bags mounted either on top of it or via a set of links for added leverage. The front is typically an upper and lower control arm situation, and bags go between the frame and the lower arm.

Front-wheel-drive and all-wheel-drive cars and trucks are different. Today's vehicles don't have a straight axle mounted under the front clip with a pair of leaf springs. Instead, they have struts and half shafts. It's a much different system overall.

In the past, this meant that you had to get very creative with the way you made everything function. It wasn't uncommon to see holes or bubbles in the hood of a Honda with the airbags mated to the upper control arms. It wasn't a pretty or lasting solution, but it was a way to bag your car.

Today, that's no longer a problem. You can buy off-the-shelf kits for a wide variety of cars from Hondas to Teslas. These strut bags (as they're called) are built to bolt into your existing suspension. Some have threaded shafts so you can decide how low or high you want the vehicle to sit, while others are very simple and just get the car low.

Cars present another series of problems, however, if you want to get truly on the ground. They likely have half shafts, which are the connections between the drive wheels and transmission. You might have to notch the body for those half shafts so that you can get the car low enough. In addition, you may have to notch the strut towers to clear the tires or upper control arms. Again, this is personal

This Honda Civic was built in the mid-1990s and featured an airbag mounted to the top of the upper control arm and a custom subframe under the hood. It worked, but it wasn't the best-looking way to do things. Fortunately, things have improved greatly since then.

preference. You don't have to go nuts notching things out. All of it comes down to how low you want to go and then cutting accordingly.

This is because modern cars by and large are unibody vehicles. That's different from most trucks in that they have a body-on-frame construction. A unibody means that the entire vehicle is the frame. Any modifications from a sunroof to a notch for the half shaft can affect how the body functions. If you do too much, you risk compromising the integrity of the vehicle in an accident, and that could be life threatening.

All of this is to say that you should make sure to take proper precautions once you start bagging your front-wheel-drive or all-wheel-drive vehicle. If you find that the chassis is flexing too much, consider tightening

Notice how tight the clearance is between the air strut and the half shaft on this Dodge Charger Hellcat. It clears, but there's not a lot of wiggle room. (Photo Courtesy Lonnie Thompson)

it up with strut tower bars, braces, or even a roll cage. It's all up to you.

As has been mentioned in previous chapters, all struts aren't created equal, so do your due diligence before dropping a wad of cash on a purchase. Similarly, they all have different applications and not just for the vehicle type. Some are made for people who want performance with the airbags. These are the guys who want to throw their cars into the corners regularly and tune their suspensions accordingly. Other setups are made for comfort so that the rider never wonders if he or she is in his or her car or a 1970s Cadillac. Whichever lane you fall into, make sure to get the right setup for you.

BAGGING A 1958 CHEVROLET IMPALA

Up to this point, you've seen many different types of installs. However, sometimes it's worth it to watch everything get done from top to bottom and see how it works in the real world when a bone-stock car is turned into something cool and bagged. That's what's going on in this chapter.

Switch Suspension has a customer with an affinity for classic Chevys, and he picked up a beautiful 1958 Impala and sent it to Switch to make it prettier. The plan was to use RideTech parts to set the car lower, install new 14-inch wheels, and use the AccuAir eLevel+ for air management with a pair of AccuAir Endo-VT tanks. It's the ultimate setup for this particular vehicle.

You may not own a car like this, but the point is to show exactly what you can do to your own ride with the right resources. It could take longer to accomplish, and you might need different parts. However, the results are worth it.

This is the project car: a 1958 Impala with a tri-tone interior, fender skirts, a spare tire kit, and jet black paint.

The Impala must've gone through a recent restoration because everything on and under the car was in flawless shape. Every nut and bolt came off without lubricant, and there was no visible rust.

Installing the Front Suspension

Chevrolet used a very similar suspension setup for many years, and only recently made adjustments. The unequal-length control arm setup paired with a frame is an excellent candidate for airbags. On a car like this, it's important to do things right. Otherwise, you risk the safety of the driver, passengers, and other people on the road.

Before starting anything, it's a good idea to lay out all of your parts to ensure that you have everything you need. This is the RideTech kit for the 1958 Impala, and it has everything required to get the Impala sitting lower.

Front Suspension Disassembly

1 *These cars come with drum brakes all the way around from the factory, but someone down the line upgraded the front clip to run disc brakes. Some of these kits push out the wheels an extra inch, and there was a little of that on this car, it just wasn't as extreme (only about 1/4 to 1/2 inch).*

2 *Once the car is on the lift, James from Switch Suspension begins taking apart the front end. He starts by removing the cotter pins on both the upper and lower ball joints and the tie-rod ends.*

4 *Separating the tie-rod ends from the spindle takes some force, usually with a heavy hammer.*

3 *The shock comes out next. There's a bolt on the top of the frame by the upper control arm that goes first, and then the two lower bolts on the lower control arm follow. It slides right out through the bottom of the arm.*

5 *With both the lower and upper ball joint nuts loosened but not removed, James takes a jack and places it under the lower control arm. Then, he uses a sledgehammer to break the lower control arm ball joint loose. The jack and the nut stops them from separating completely, and allows him to remove the coil in a more controlled fashion.*

6 Now that the ball joints are free, James takes the entire spindle assembly, including the brakes, off the control arms. He uses a heavy-duty cable tie to hold it against the frame so that the brake lines don't stretch or break.

7 Using the jack, James slowly relieves pressure on the lower control arm. Eventually, there's no more pressure on the spring, and he can just pull it out.

8 The lower control arm bolts to the frame via a cross shaft. Once it's unbolted, James can pull it down and set it to the side.

9 *The upper control arm takes a little bit more finagling to access, as the Impala has a big-block V-8 under the hood. It's important to save the original shims, so once the arm is loosened, James pulls them off and sets them aside.*

10 *With the cross shafts unbolted, the upper control arm is now free and ready for removal.*

Prepping the Front Airbags

With the frame now clear of any parts, it's time to install the front cups for the airbags.

1 *This is the inside of the frame where the spring used to sit. If you look to the left, you'll see a hole. Just to the right of that hole is where James is going to run the air line so that it goes through the frame, exiting toward the middle of the body.*

2 *After applying a bit of Loctite, James installs the fitting into the airbag. The top half of the fitting swivels, so it's not critical that it's lined up in any particular way.*

3 *After test fitting the upper cup in the frame, James makes a mark on it. The idea is to make an access hole for the air line on the cup so that it can run through the frame properly.*

4 *Now, he uses a hole saw to make the cut. Once it's done, he uses a file to clean and deburr the edges so that the air line won't get cut along the way.*

5 *With the cup now bolted onto the bag for good, a piece of all-thread is installed as well. This locates the cup in the stock shock mount and provides a way to bolt the cup in place on the chassis.*

6 *Here's the completed bag assembly for the front. Notice how the fitting is pointing toward the hole and how the cup is mounted to the bag, slightly offset. This is to give the bag ample clearance in the spring pocket.*

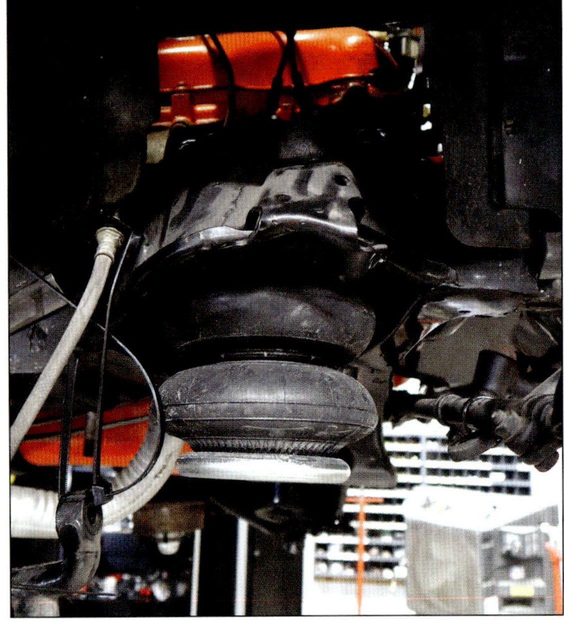

7. *The bag is then bolted into the frame. Although it will still come out before it's in there for good, it's important that it's in place now so that James can check for clearances.*

Installing the Front Shock Mounts

Shocks are an important safety feature on any vehicle, but in the case of this 1958 Impala (and many other vehicles), they can't go into the stock location once airbags are installed. Instead, use a shock relocation kit, such as this one, to place the shock outside of the control arm.

2. *Cutting out the fender liner precisely takes an air saw and patience. It's the most clean way to get the cut, but it's quite loud.*

3. *Cleaning up the edges from the cut happens quickly with an angle grinder and a sanding disc.*

1. *The stock metal fender liner is still in place on the Impala, but it's in the way of the shock mount. Using the shock relocation kit as a reference, James traces out a wide amount from the fender well to give the shock plenty of room.*

5 *The hardware provided with the kit includes these bolts with self-tapping grooves. They tap the frame as they go in and cinch up.*

4 *Now, with the shock relocation kit set in place, James uses a marker to show where he needs to drill holes. He'll then use a center punch and drill to get the job done.*

6 *The bolts are put into the holes using an impact wrench. The bottom one is done last to provide extra pressure against the frame.*

Installing the Lower Control Arms

The new lower control arms from RideTech go on the same way as the stock models with just a few differences.

1 *After putting in the new frame bolts, the lower control arm is lifted up to connect to the frame.*

2 *The bolt that's farthest toward the rear of the Impala secures it in place. The most forward connection is made with a billet block and two bolts. All of the hardware comes with the kit.*

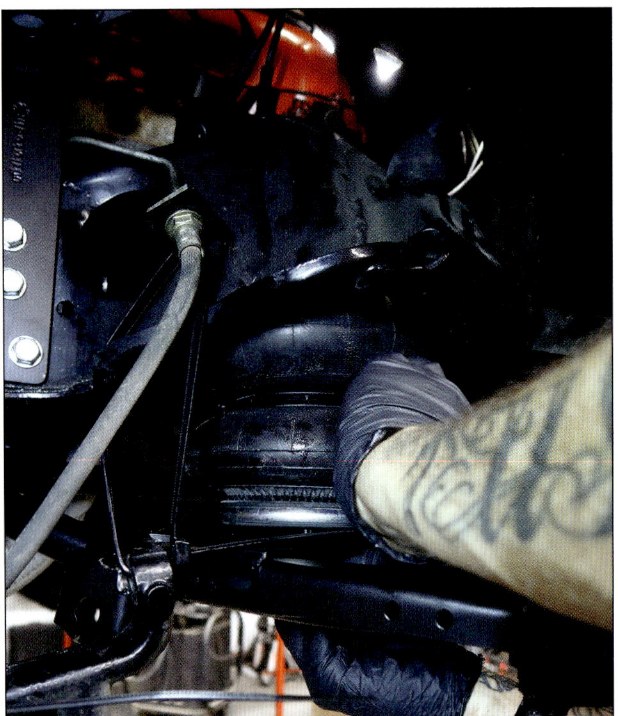

4 *A set of steering stops are installed later as well. These help limit the turning radius on the car, which ensures that the wheel won't hit the shock.*

3 *Once James lifts the lower control arm in place, he's able to bolt the bottom of the airbag to the lower control arm. This is what keeps the airbag in the right place at all times.*

Installing the Upper Control Arms

The upper control arms go in just as easily as the lowers, except first you have to mount a new ball joint.

1 *The new ball joints for the RideTech upper control arms bolt right in. What's nice is that if you ever need a replacement set, you can pick them up at a local parts shop.*

2 *The RideTech arm bolts in place using new hardware and the factory shims. The car will need an alignment later, but for now, it's set up with the original shims.*

3 *Now the factory spindle is ready for reinstallation. After hoisting it up and bolting in the lower ball joint, the upper is loosely assembled. New cotter pins come next.*

Installing the Front Shocks

Now that the suspension is assembled, the shocks come next.

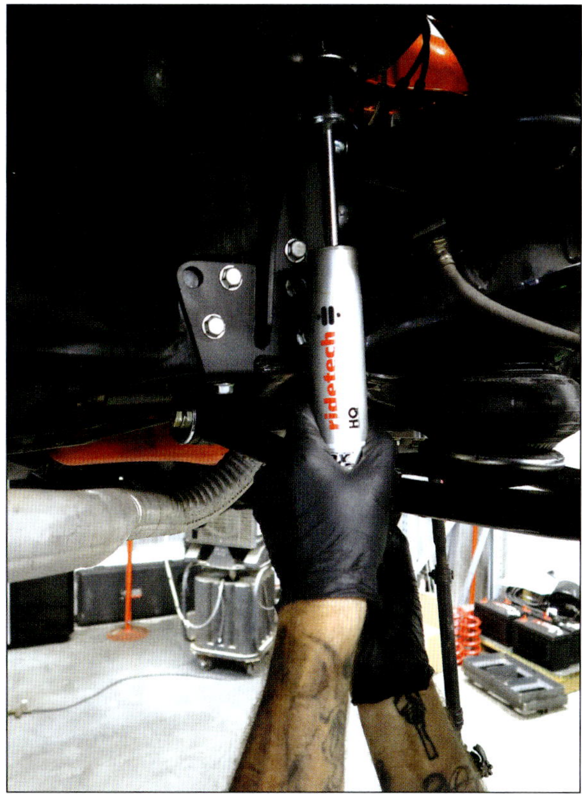

1 *Installing the top of the front shock is fairly straightforward. Just make sure the bushings and washers are in the right sequence and then bolt it down.*

2 *The bottom part of the shock bolts to the lower control arm.*

Installing the Sway Bar

Although the Impala had a sway bar already, the RideTech kit came with a beefier model.

1 *Before the tie-rod ends were reinstalled onto the spindles, the new sway bar was routed through the steering system.*

2 *The new sway bar has shims to help you place it in the right spot. It's installed loosely using the provided hardware.*

3 *The sway-bar end links are bolted to the mounts on the lower control arms. Then, the bolts are tightened.*

Installing the Rear Suspension

The rear suspension on the 1958 Impala is great for airbags. There's an upper wishbone, two trailing arms, shocks, and coils. Removing everything takes a few hours. Then, it's ready for bags.

Rear Suspension Disassembly

1 *The stock rear suspension was recently refreshed, which meant that disassembling it would be fairly easy.*

2 *The shocks come off first. They're held in place with bolts on both ends, and once they're off, they're placed to the side.*

3 *All it takes to remove the springs is to lower down the stands to release the pressure. Then, just pull them out.*

4 *The upper wishbone comes off next. First, it's unbolted from the top of the axle and then from the frame mounts. There are shims behind there too, so they're set aside for use with the replacement wishbone.*

5 *There are two mounts left on the wishbone, and they need to go on the new arm. Placing them side-by-side, James swaps them out.*

6 *Taking out the rear trailing arms takes two bolts per side: one up front, and one connecting the arm to the axle.*

7 *The axle mount for the trailing arm utilizes this special bolt that also holds the shock in place. James made sure to keep this handy, as the kit did not come with a replacement.*

8 *The upper bump stops also have to come off. This is easily done with a ratcheting wrench.*

Prepping the Rear Airbags

1 *This picture was taken looking up into the spring mount. The brass-colored panel on the right is what was left of the bump stop. The RideTech suspension kit keys into the bump stop mount and the spring cup to keep it stable.*

2 *The new rear bag mounts bolt to the bump stop and use a piece of all-thread so that the mounts don't twist. Once they're test fitted in place, a spot is marked to drill for the all-thread.*

3 The hole is drilled for the all-thread using progressively larger bits.

4 Back at the bench, the rear bag cups are prepped with the all-thread.

5 Just like up front, the fittings first receive some Loctite. Then, they're installed into the airbag.

6 The assembly is complete once the cup is bolted to the bag.

7 The rear mount is put in place, and where the original bump stop mounted to the frame, a new one is set in its place. The aluminum spacer may get cut down later, but for now, it's in a good spot. That aluminum spacer also holds part of the bag bracket in place.

8 The bottom of the bags bolt to the mounts on the trailing arms. Now, the airbags are officially installed.

9 Last on the list are the rear shocks. They mount using the factory hardware.

10 After a little silicone spray is applied to the end, some 1/4-inch soft line is pushed into the PTC fitting on the airbag.

11 To secure the line in place, James uses a screw and a plastic line clamp.

Installing the Rear Suspension

1 *The RideTech upper wishbone bolts in place using the factory hardware and shims. If they decide they need to tweak the pinion angle later, they can just mess with the shims to get it to the right spot.*

2 *The new RideTech trailing arms bolt into the factory positions using the factory hardware. It doesn't get much easier than that.*

3 *On the axle side, James uses the same shock bolt that came from the factory. It's keyed, so he makes sure it's sitting properly before securing it in place.*

Clearance Issues

Every vehicle is different, and there is no blanket statement that covers all of the things you may encounter during a bag job that can cause you problems. In the course of doing the installation on the 1958 Impala, a few issues popped up that were specific to this car. They'll be addressed before it's shipped back to the customer, but, as usual, the team at Switch Suspension has a plan.

Anything that sits lower than the frame on a vehicle needs to be sorted out. In this case, the issues mostly appear around the exhaust. The passenger's side sits too low up front, which means once the car is laid out, it could be the part that keeps it from dropping fully.

In this case, they built a new exhaust. That way, they could route it exactly the way they want.

Those are the only issues that were run into on this particular vehicle; but remember, every car is different, and yours will have its own share of clearance concerns.

Installing Air Suspension

Getting the air suspension part of things done is a multistage process. It starts with the plumbing and then moves on from there.

If you look at the left side of the image, you'll see the passenger-side exhaust hanging lower than the lower control arms. That makes them the lowest point on the vehicle, and that can be a problem.

The exhaust also sits perilously close to the rear airbags. The heat and vibration from the pipe could contact the airbag and cause it to melt and rupture.

Routing the Front Air Lines

With the front suspension complete, it was time to run the new air line.

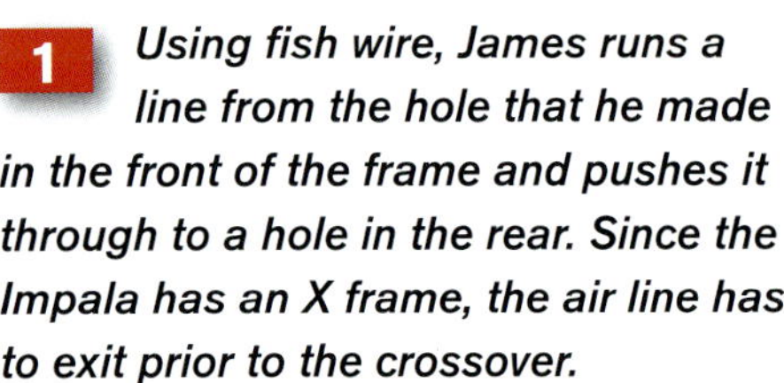

1 *Using fish wire, James runs a line from the hole that he made in the front of the frame and pushes it through to a hole in the rear. Since the Impala has an X frame, the air line has to exit prior to the crossover.*

2 *Next, he tapes the new 1/4-inch air line to the fish line so that he can pull it through the frame. He leaves a lot of excess line so that he has options to work with later.*

3 *Before installing the line into the fitting on the airbag, he applies some braided sleeving over it. This provides an extra bit of protection to the line just in case it rubs against something during use.*

4 *The guys at Switch Suspension use silicone spray on their air lines prior to installing them into a fitting. It provides a little bit of lubrication, which helps the line get into the fitting without roughing anything up.*

5 *The braided line is visible through this hole in the frame. It's now mounted to the airbag and ready for connection on the other side.*

6 *You must keep plastic air lines away from heat, and the exhaust is an obvious source. Since clearance is so tight underneath the car, the team routes the line where the brake lines go, using high-end cable ties to zip them into place.*

Tips for Installing AccuAir Height Sensors

One of the key parts to the AccuAir system is its height sensors. When installed properly, they give the ECU the information it needs to automatically adjust the height of the vehicle. Mounting them can be daunting though, as you don't want to do things multiple times, and sometimes it's hard to get parts mated together. However, once it's done right, it's like magic.

This is the sensor itself. Just to the left of the four screws in the sensor is a piece of plastic that helps you determine the overall range of travel for the arm. Basically, there is 100 degrees of motion from all the way up to all the way down to work with.

AccuAir's instructions say to use double-sided tape to temporarily place the sensor, but the guys at Switch made up this tool instead. The circular base contains a magnet, and the arms fit into an AccuAir height sensor mount.

When assembled on a sensor, the magnet lets you move it all over your chassis in the hunt for that perfect spot. Consider using something like this on your own build, as it might make your life easier.

Installing the Front Height Sensors

1 *There aren't many good options for mounting the height sensors on the Impala. Under the hood was considered, but the big-block V-8 made space and heat a problem. In the end, the team decided to mount it off the chassis and the shock absorber.*

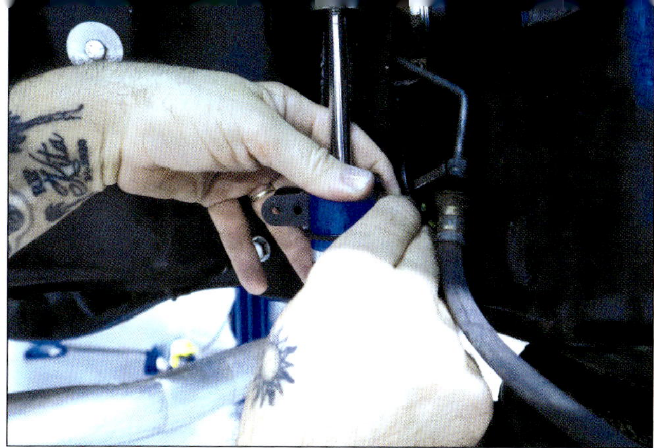

2 *Switch Suspension sells these cool height sensor mount clamps made by Choppin' Block Chassis Products. They come in various sizes and are designed to go around link bars and other round objects. In this case, they went around the shock absorbers, which were temporarily protected by some blue tape during the mockup phase.*

3 *James used his magnetic test base to simulate how it would go on the shock relocation kit. After testing, it was determined to be a go.*

4 *Once the linkage was trimmed, the height sensor was mounted on the shock relocation kit.*

5 *Once everything tested okay, the sensor was permanently installed and good to go.*

Installing the Rear Height Sensors

1 *Using the magnetic base as a starting point, the height sensor is placed on the frame and mocked up. James cycles the suspension to make sure that the linkage moves smoothly throughout the range of travel and it won't overextend and cause problems.*

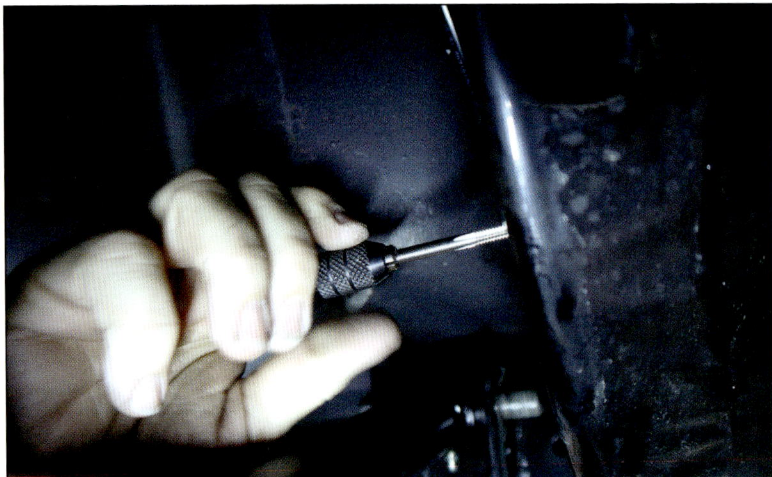

2 *With the suspension raised up all the way, James makes a mark on the trailing arm and the height sensor using chalk. This tells him where the center of his arm needs to go and where on the trailing arm the linkage needs to sit.*

3 *Once the height sensor is in the right spot, the frame is marked, drilled, and tapped to accept bolts. Then, the sensor is bolted in place.*

4 *Here they used the same Choppin' Block Chassis Products clamps like they used on the front shocks. This time, they go around the tubular trailing arms.*

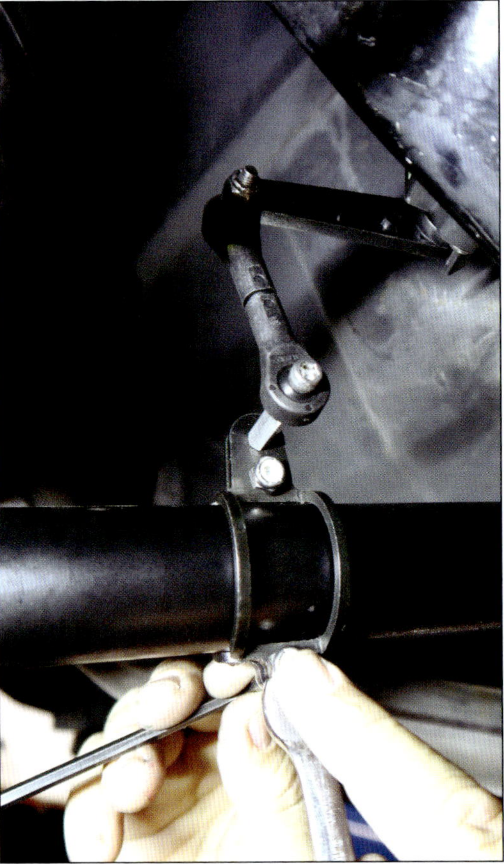

5 *Once the sensor linkage is cut down, it's bolted to the sensor and the mount. Then, the suspension is cycled to ensure the sensor doesn't bind.*

Re-Clocking AccuAir Height Sensors

Because you have to mount the AccuAir height sensors in very particular locations, sometimes you may find yourself in a scenario where the wiring harness isn't in a good place. Maybe it's pointing directly at the frame or it's just not clear of something that's hot. Many times, the solution is as simple as re-clocking the height sensor arm. ■

If you look close at the center of the arm, you'll see four screws and one center pivot. The center pivot has a flat side on one end. This means that you can unscrew the arm and re-clock it by rotating it at 90-degree intervals. What you have to do is make sure that flat side always points away from the sensor connector. If you move it, you won't get an accurate reading.

Fixing the issue is fairly straightforward. First, unscrew the height sensor arm from the body.

Now, lift the arm vertically off of the body, making sure not to move the flat spot in relation to the sensor connector.

Re-Clocking AccuAir Height Sensors *continued*

Reattach the sensor arm in its new position, making sure the flat spot stays in the proper orientation.

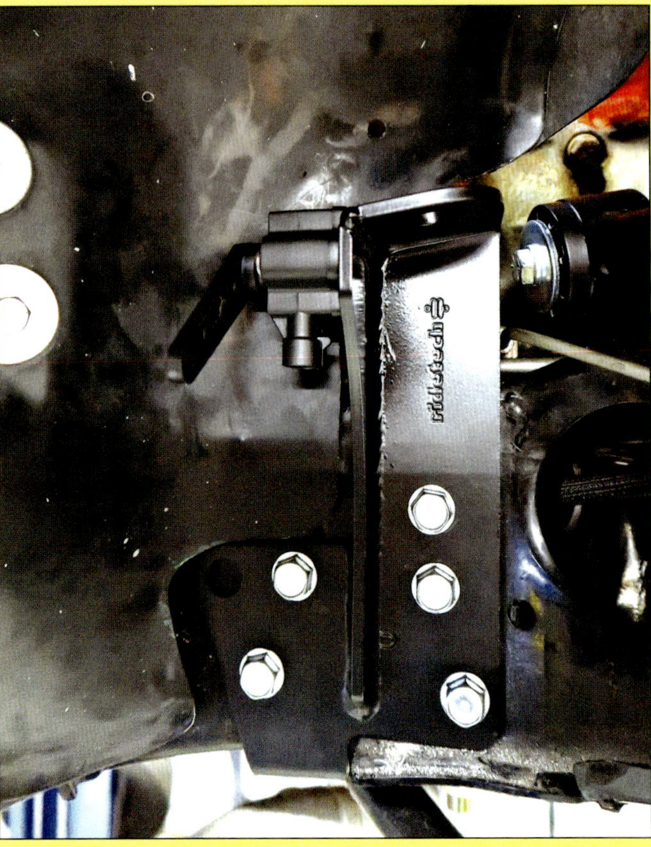

Now, the sensor connector is pointed down and away from the frame, but the arm still has the range of travel needed to work properly.

Building the Air Management System

The trunk of the 1958 Impala was ready for air management, but there were questions about how it should look. Is it better to hide all of the components, or should they be shown off? Do they choose one 5-gallon tank or two 3-gallon tanks? There were a lot of decisions to make.

Fortunately, the crew at Switch Suspension has all of these parts in stock, so they were able to open a few boxes and toy around with ideas.

1 *The idea began with the debate between tanks. No matter what, they would run an AccuAir Endo-VT, which is an air tank with the valves built in. However, it took some testing to figure out whether a single 5-gallon tank or two 3-gallon tanks was better.*

2 James played around with a few things and came up with this concept: two tanks flanked by Viair compressors with the AccuAir eLevel+ ECU mounted in the middle. Everything would go in a custom box and would eventually be covered by a false floor made by the stereo shop that was going to work on the car next.

3 He took a bunch of measurements for the box and then went off to the store to buy some MDF.

4 With everything laid out on the wood, James began cutting out the panels.

5 Eventually, after a lot of screwing and gluing, the box took shape.

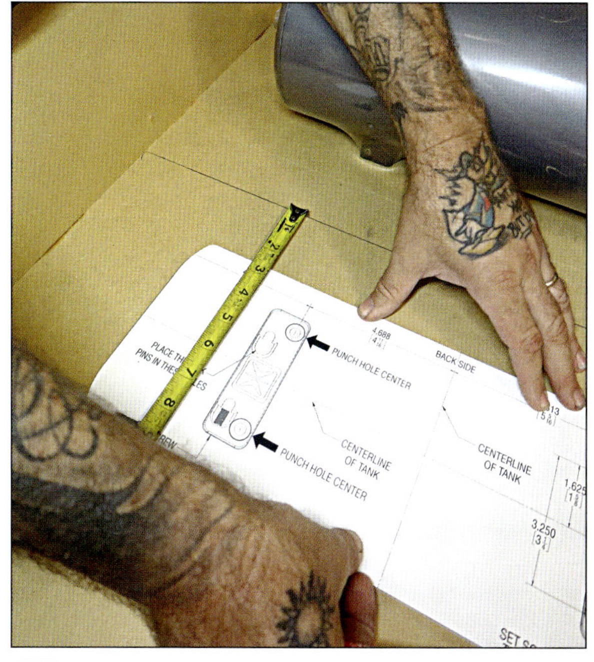

6 The Endo-VT tanks come with plastic templates that make the installation process go smoothly. Once everything was assembled, James marked everything for the tanks. He had to flip the mounts on one so they would both have the valves exiting on the same side, but it was an easy fix.

7 *After some carpet work and some trim, this was the working setup. The tanks now sat in a curved valley in the middle of the box with the compressors and tanks on the same plane.*

Plumbing the Air Management System

1 *With everything in place, the fittings were mocked up as well. Nothing was permanent at this stage, as the tanks would be painted to match the car later on.*

2 *Here's the first piece of hard line, which runs from the compressor to the tank and includes the check valve.*

3 *A combination of bulkhead fittings and reducers are mounted through the box. The idea is to run the lines out of the valves at one end of the box to the outside, then back in, run toward the ECU and dive under it, back up, and out the other side of the box. It sounds more complex than it is, and it looks really cool.*

4 *Here's the partial result (minus one tank).*

5 *The ECU connects to a bunch of harnesses, which means that wiring has to come into the box. Fortunately, that was already planned, so it was run through a hole in the side.*

6 *The wiring is fed up and through the box so that it's ready to plug into the ECU. Each harness is different, so there's no way to confuse them.*

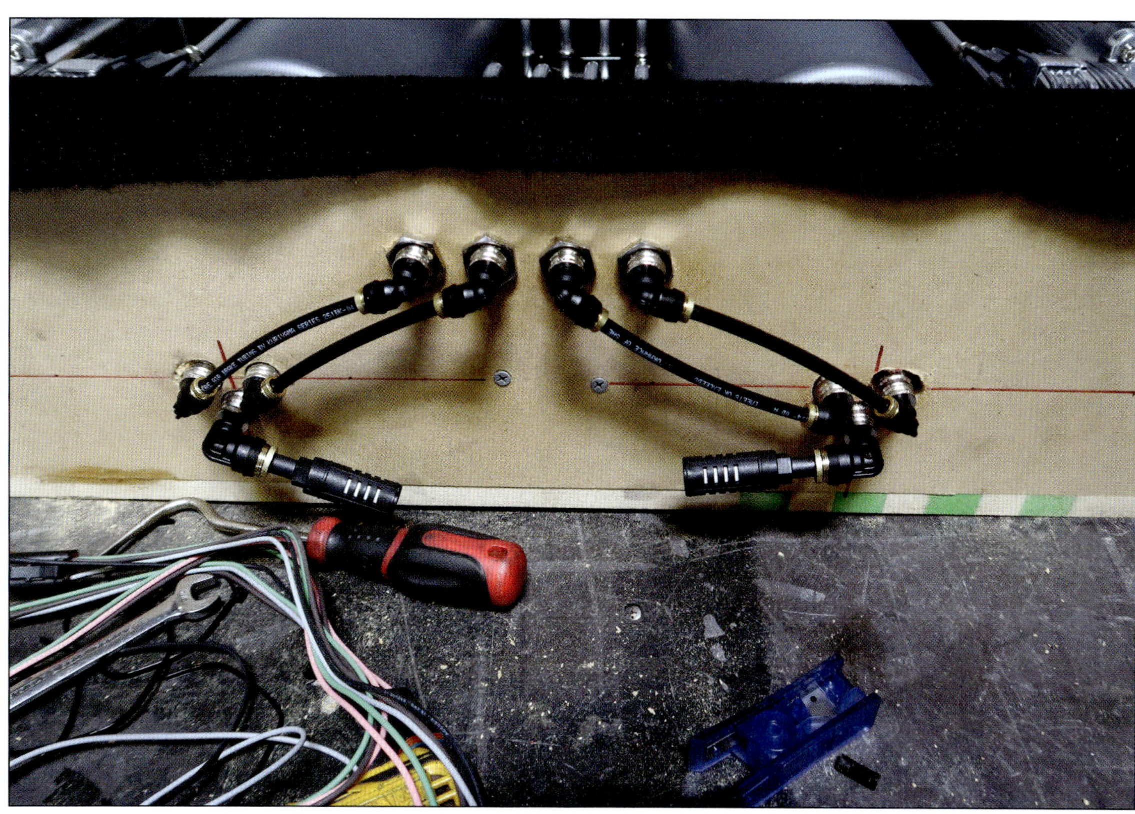

7 *Here's what the air connections look like on the back of the box. This will all be covered by the trim panels from the stereo shop.*

Running the Height Sensor Wiring

Once the wiring is complete to the ECU, run the harnesses out to the corners themselves. Each sensor is labelled, but it can get a bit tricky.

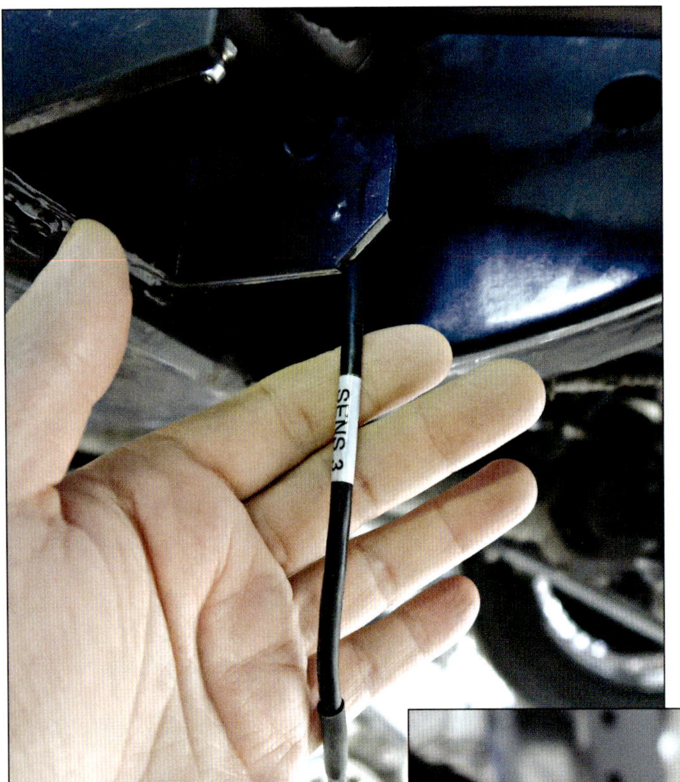

1 *This is one of the sensor wires labelled "Sensor 3." It's been run next to the air lines, but there's some extra slack in the wire.*

2 *Use a height sensor trim kit. Switch Suspension sells these for $20, and they have enough clips and pins in there to do a complete car. You can also get the tool you need to crimp the lines if necessary.*

3 *After cutting the wiring to length, the connector is taken to the bench. The orange cap on the harness pulls right off, and you can remove the original pins from the connector with a pointed tool.*

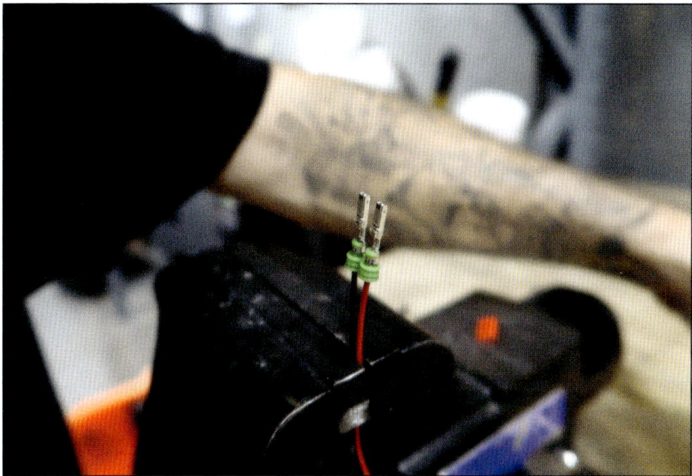

4 *Now, crimp the connectors so they go around the green weather-tight seals on the wiring. Then, once you confirm that you have the right color sequence, push the pins into the connector until they click. Reinstall the orange cap, and you're done.*

5 *The kit comes with heat shrink so that you can tighten up that connection too. Now, there's no excess wiring to worry about.*

The Completed Air Management Setup

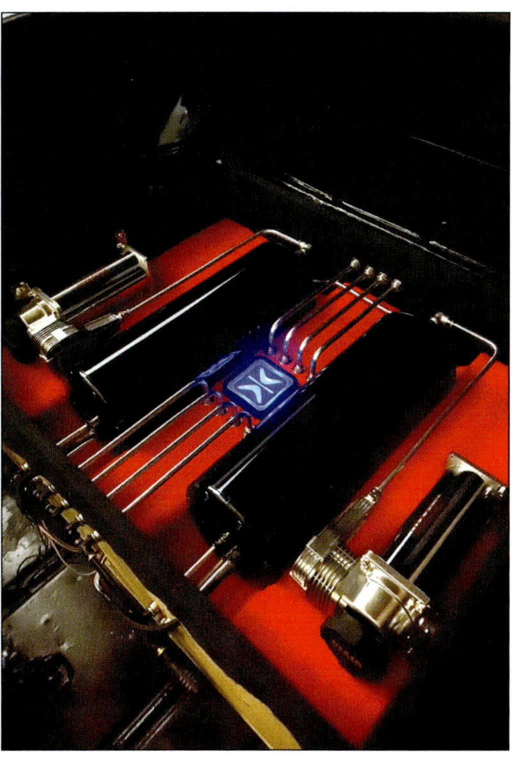

1 *With the tanks and compressors painted, hard lines polished, new carpet laid, and everything ready to go, the completed setup looks amazing.*

2 *The team decided toward the end to redo the floor of the box in red carpet to match the interior of the Impala. The ECU also cycles through colors, giving it a nice effect.*

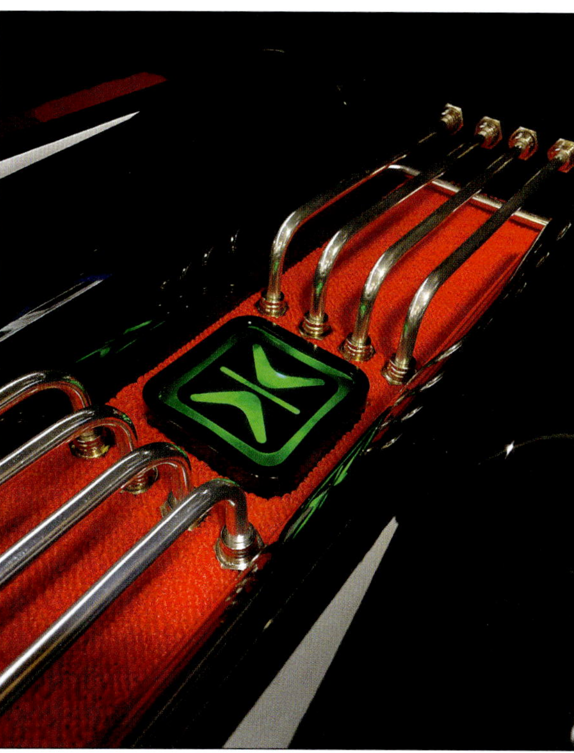

Programming the ECU

Once everything is connected and good to go, it's time to program the ECU. AccuAir has a detailed manual that explains how it all works, but the general idea is to use the controller to start the process, and most of it is done for you from there forward.

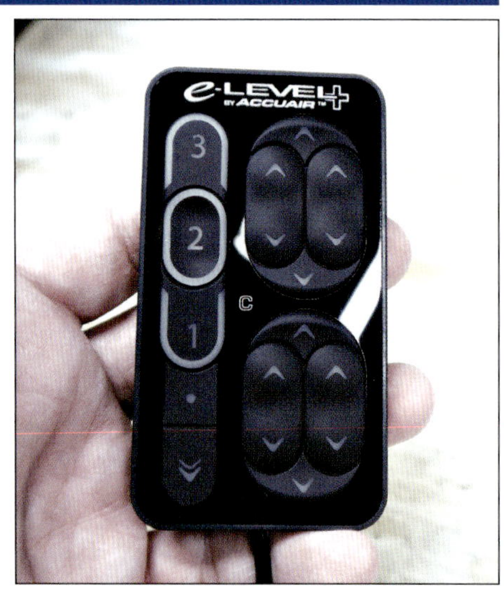

This is the AccuAir eLevel+ controller. It connects via a USB port, and you can mount it wherever you like in your car or just keep it loose. See the little dot below the number "1"? If you hold the dot button and the "1" button at the same time, it starts the calibration process.

The calibration process involves the system moving the car up and down, dancing each corner around as it determines where the car should be. Once it's complete, the car is ready to drive.

Here's the result: a laid-out 1958 Impala on 14-inch reverse wheels. Now, it's on to the stereo shop for some more goodies.

AccuAir
200 Sea Ray Dr.
Merritt Island, FL 32953
833-247-3696
accuair.com
Email: sales@accuair.com

Air Lift Performance
800-248-0892
airliftperformance.com

Air Zenith
3651 W. Ali Baba Ln.
Suite 107
Las Vegas, NV 89118
702-270-7988
air-zenith.com

Arizona High Test
6948 W. Chandler Blvd.
Suite #2
Chandler, AZ 85226
480-640-5755
arizonahightest.com
Instagram: @
 arizona_high_test

Ashcroft
250 E. Main St.
Stratford, CT 06614
203-378-8281
ashcroft.com

Autometer
413 W. Elm St.
Sycamore, IL 60178
866-248-6357
autometer.com

AVS
4555 N. Cedar Ave.
Fresno, CA 93726
559-486-5444
avsontheweb.com

Bag Riders
208 Flynn Ave. Suite 2C
Burlington, VT 05401
844-404-7344
bagriders.com

BellTech
300 W. Pontiac Way
Clovis, CA 93612
800-445-3767
belltech.com

Carolina Kustoms
6600 N.E. Columbia Blvd.
Portland, OR 97218
503-954-1369
carolinakustoms.com

Choppin' Block Chassis
 Products
5575 W. Barstow Ave.
Fresno, CA 93722
559-275-2901
cbcpro.com

Chris Alston's Chassisworks
8661 Younger Creek Dr.
Sacramento, CA 95828
888-388-0297
cachassisworks.com

Continental
continental-industry.com

Cool Cars Engineering
7514 Preston Hwy.
Louisville, KY 40219
502-969-7600
coolcars.org

D2 Racing
2435 S. Alston Ave.
Durham, NC 27713
919-544-4171
d2racing.com

Dakota Digital
4510 W. 61st St. N.
Sioux Falls, SD 57107
605-332-6513
dakotadigital.com

Dino's Chevy Only
dinoschevyonly.shop

Firestone
800-888-0650
firestoneip.com

Flo Airride Mfg.
951-249-6478
floairride.com

Frontier Shop Supplies
4551 E. Ivy St. #101
Mesa, AZ 85205
480-981-1126
frontiershopsupplies.com

GlowShift Gauges
444 Commerce Ln. Suite A
West Berlin, NJ, 08091
856-768-8300
glowshiftdirect.com

Grainger
800-472-4643
grainger.com

Grunion Customs
13011 N. Cave Creek Rd.
Phoenix, AZ 85022
602-258-0088
grunionfabrication.com

Heidts
800 Oakwood Rd.
Lake Zurich, IL 60047
800-841-8188
heidts.com

KP Components
8661 Younger Creek Dr.
Sacramento, CA 95828
888-388-0299
kpcomponents.com

Kwix UK
330 Four Oaks Rd.
Walton Summit
Preston, PR5 8AP
United Kingdom
01772-695-697
kwixuk.com

Little Shop Mfg.
150 Mahr Ave.
Lawrenceburg, TN 38464
littleshopmfg.com

Lowboy Motorsports
1045 W. Broadway Rd.
Suite 4
Mesa, AZ 85210
480-717-9256
lowboymotorsports.com

McGaughys
4603 E. Vine Ave.
Fresno, CA 93725
559-226-8196
mcgaughys.com

Metalox Fabrication
8615 W. Kelton Ln.
Suite 305
Peoria, AZ 85382
623-308-1170
Instagram: @metaloxfab

NotcHead
30229 US 2
Sultan, WA 98294
360-243-3492
notchead.com

Oasis Manufacturing
23011 Alcalde Dr. Suite P
Laguna Hills, CA 92653
888-966-2747
oasismfg.com

Only Charged Dubs
Unit 2B Railway Ct.
Sandall Stones Rd.
Kirk Sandall Ind. Est.
Doncaster
DN3 1QR
United Kingdom
01302-885310
onlychargeddubs.co.uk

Parker
800-272-7537
parker.com

RideTech
350 S. St. Charles St.
Jasper, IN 47546
812-481-4787
ridetech.com

Rigid Tools
400 Clark St.
Elyria, OH 44035
800-474-3443
ridgid.com

Slam Specialties
5845 E. Terrace Ave.
Fresno, CA 93727
888-352-5225
slamspecialties.com

SMC Pneumatics
3810 Prospect Ave. Unit A
Yorba Linda, CA 92886
714-312-5419
smcpneumatics.com

Swagelok
swagelok.com

Switch Suspension
2150 W. Broadway Rd.
#102
Mesa, AZ 85202
800-928-1984
switchsuspension.com

Toyo Tire & Rubber Company
toyotires.com

Tuckers Classic Auto Parts
800-544-1955
tuckersparts.com

Universal Air Suspension
463 W. Highland Ave.
San Bernardino, CA 92405
800-864-2470
universalair.com

Viair
15 Edelman
Irvine, CA 92618
949-585-0011
viaircorp.com